Practicing

THE POWER
OF PRESENT
MOMENT

Practicing

THE POWER
OF PRESENT
MOMENT

SANJEEV KUMAR

iUniverse

Practicing the Power of Present Moment

iUniverse books may be ordered through booksellers or by contacting:

iUniverse
1663 Liberty Drive
Bloomington, IN 47403
www.iuniverse.com
1-800-Authors (1-800-288-4677)

ISBN: 978-1-4917-7880-7 (sc)
ISBN: 978-1-4917-7881-4 (e)

Library of Congress Control Number: 2015953749

Print information available on the last page.

iUniverse rev. date: 12/28/2015

This book is dedicated to

Sri Nand Kishore Prasad Singh (my father) and Srimati Shanti Devi (my mother), who brought light from darkness and showed me the path of wisdom, knowledge, and truth.

I am really proud of my father, who struggled his entire life to teach me honesty, integrity, and humanity.

"Meditation brings wisdom, creativity, and death of ego."-
Sanjeev Kumar

CONTENTS

INTRODUCTION:
CELEBRATE EACH MOMENT

There are two ways to live our lives; the first way is mind, and the other way is awareness. The people who live through mind always think, because mind means thinking. Awareness means we are just noticing, observing, and witnessing whatever is happening around us but we are not judging and labeling them. It is very true that we cannot live every moment in the now! Another meaning of mind is to live in the past and the future.

Most people are trying to bring the past and the future into this moment because they live with mind in the form of flashback, memory, anxiety, projection, dream, imagination etc. but we cannot live in the past. Can we laugh in the past? No, we cannot, because the past is already gone, but we can reconnect the past to this moment by living right now. We can laugh only right now and here, but through memory, while viewing photographs, for example, we can connect with the beautiful moments of past events with family members and friends.

When I look back at myself in the past, I remember that I suffered in silence because I was living in memory, dream, imagination, projection etc. when I was in school. My performance was no better than that of other students because I used to live in the past, thinking about sports, games, and movies while the teacher was trying to teach us. I was never focused at all in the now. There were a few other students who did well because they were totally present in that moment. They were witnessing, watchful, alert, and aware of those thoughts and followed what the teacher taught them. My lack of attention to the now affected my performance badly. Later on, I realized that living in memory, dream, and imagination ruins our lives.

There are millions of people who aren't living in the now because they are living only through mind, not with awareness. My intention is to help those people who are not living in the now.

When we talk to people, most of them talk from their mind about living in the past or the future. Everyone has ego. We cannot live without it, but too much ego is not good for us. When children are born, they do not have ego at all; but as soon as they start learning from their parents, family members, and society, they begin developing ego, which is good. Later on as they get older, their mind get conditioned and programmed with beliefs, rituals, dogmas etc. and they develop too much ego, which is not good. A little bit of ego, which includes self-respect, self-image, self-esteem etc. is needed. Without it, we cannot exist; human life is not possible without ego.

In this book, I am sharing my thoughts regarding living an aware, mindful life filled with the joy of celebrating each and every moment, whether it is painful or blissful. Every moment is new and fresh for us, so we must live our lives to the fullest potential.

We are very busy in our lives, so we need to take deep and relaxed breaths and enjoy each second as it comes in order to get rid of negative emotions. There is always positivity and light waiting for us, but we often do not observe them. When we live here in the now, they are already here.

Trust

Create a huge amount of trust within yourself, and then existence will take care of you no matter what happens. If you would look back and investigate yourself in this moment, you would find that nothing wrong ever happened in your life and nothing wrong will take place in the future, because everything happens for a good reason, but you need to be honest, truthful, pure, and internally cleansed as much as you can be by looking inside in order to live in the now—and then everything will fall into the right place.

If this now is okay, then the next now is also okay

"The deeper meaning of life is to understand wholeness, completeness, and fullness."-Sanjeev Kumar

CHAPTER 1

Living in the Now

Being in this moment is the starting point of your life

All human beings have a tremendous amount of power to do anything they want in their lives, but they often cannot discover that power because they are full of thoughts of desires, ego, wants, attachments etc. These thoughts fill up with thoughts of the past and the future, which separate us from reality. Reality is present at the center of being, but most of us are present on the circumference, where we start thinking about others by missing the now. This now is called "the divine moment" because it takes control of the past and the future and helps us to get rid of all kinds of negative emotions and problems. It uncovers our true human potential.

It is the moment of discovery

Most of the great discoveries happen in this moment. Newton discovered gravitational force by just noticing the falling of an apple from a tree. There must have been millions of people before Newton, who had seen the falling of an apple from a tree, but none of them were

1

aware and noticed it, but he just noticed, witnessed, and discovered it.

How can we control memory, imagination, dream, and projection?

There is only way to control the past and the future, and that is by living right *now*. In fact, being present is the greatest gift we will ever have. We cannot observe the real thoughts of now if we are in thoughts of memory, dream, projection etc. because many of these thoughts are covering up the main and original thoughts so that we start labeling and judging the thoughts of dream, imagination, memory etc. The main powerful thoughts of this moment are hidden because we are living in illusionary thoughts of the past and the future and we are disconnected from this moment. Therefore, it is better to live here right now, and then we can observe the powerful real thoughts within and look at things as they really are. We can become witnessing, alert, watchful, and conscious of what we are doing.

A long time ago when I used to live in memory, projection, dream, and imagination, I was under control of many illusionary thoughts, and I had many problems of memory loss, short temper, distraction, anger, fear, attention loss etc. But as soon as I started living in this moment, I realized the power of *now* is here. Most of my problems have disappeared, my productivity level has gone up, and I have gotten rid of useless thoughts.

The fact is that life exists in this moment, and if you are not here right now, you have missed beautiful moments of your life.

Don't move into the past, because it is memory and everything there has already disappeared. Don't move into the future, because that is only imagination, projection, and dream, which have not yet happened. Just remain right here right now, and then all useless thoughts of the past or future disappear. The present is pure, clean, and open to the Universe, where life is eternal and full of joy. This eternal moment gets rid of all tensions, anxieties, and worries. When you are in a state of no thought, there is no past and no future; there is only the present in that thoughtless state.

Tomorrow Never Comes

What's going to happen tomorrow? This is the biggest question in our lives. Tomorrow is just an illusion created by our minds that separates us from today! There is no tomorrow. Only this moment exists here right now, but we can take control of tomorrow by living right now with focus on the awareness of breath and let go of everything; then we can know that now is the answer for the question of what will happen tomorrow. No one knows what will happen in the next moment, but when you totally relax into this moment, witnessing and being watchful of your thoughts, then the answer is already there.

Students force themselves to prepare for examinations; therefore, they work hard, but they are living in tomorrow. How can they live in this moment? Life is here right now. On the other hand, they can be highly productive when they focus right here in the now and let go of everything else. In other words, witness of tomorrow moment in this now, but never think *for* tomorrow. Students are often doing too much preparation for tomorrow, which is again an illusion because tomorrow never comes and the past is already gone. Can you laugh into the past or future? You cannot because the past has already moved into different dimensions and the future is not at your hand.

Force Creates Resistance

Parents put too much pressure on their children to become doctors, engineers, scientists etc. especially in a few Asian countries, but it is worthless to put so much pressure on them. Parents want their children to study every moment, but children cannot study each and every moment. Children want fun, enjoyment, and entertainment. Therefore, some children are committing suicide in those countries because they cannot tolerate so much pressure to study. This suicide rate continues to rise. But the point of understanding is that we cannot live in the future. As soon as you try to force children, it means you are suggesting them to handle the future moments in the now, which is not possible. Why can't we let our children to follow their passions, which are connected with heart, not with the mind? If they want to become scientists, let them do so; but we cannot force them to become doctors, professors etc. because force creates resistance within an individual and many problems are created.

We are too anxious for tomorrow, and we express this in the form of worry, which blocks opportunity, happiness, and inner joy. Worry and anxiety keep us for the next moment, which cannot be handled now. Therefore, just make this moment okay, and then the next moment is already going to be okay. Worry creates a barrier in our lives.

Worrying about what's going to happen is a negative projection of our futures. Living here right now is ultimately the best thing we can do. It helps us to build up relationships, attract abundance and opportunities, fulfill our lives, and make our lives deeper, fuller, and richer.

Internal Cleansing

Right thoughts, feelings, and intentions arise from the deepest core of being. Words, languages, and actions are meaningless because we are more connected with outside world when we live superficially, and it accumulate inside us in the form of toxins, which affect our thoughts, feelings, and intentions; gradually we can observe that we are losing true selves because we are living a dualistic pattern of life, clinging to material desires that bring pain and suffering to our lives. All attractions are temporary distractions when we live in periphery, but as soon as we move to the center of being by dissolving the ego through internal cleansing, then we can discover our true selves.

As long as we live on the periphery, we are stuck with noise and turmoil because we are confused and living in doubtful situations under the control of the ego. On the periphery, there is a collection of negative emotional energy in the form of deadly diseases like cancer and AIDS. All of these things attack us because we are living in the past and the future in the form of thoughts filled with hatred, jealousy, fear, and anger. As soon as we live here right now, we can observe that negative thought energy is dissolved, and we can discover our true selves.

Therefore, we need to go for internal cleansing, which means to focus on the awareness of breath and connect more with real nature. Try to take care of your thoughts, feelings, and right intentions by living with positive people and consuming high-vibration food, which is directly connected with existence. Go for morning walks and do meditation in order to cleanse yourself.

We can keep on collecting useless and purposeless thoughts in the form of ego. They cover up the thoughts of real being and separate us from true self because ego is delusion, full of endless desires, wants, hatred, jealousy, fear, anger etc. You are going to lose your true or higher self if you are fully occupied in the conditional mind and separated from the unconditional mind. You can observe that you are getting more connected with negative people and negative situations of life and there is no empty space left over. Finally, it destroys internal peace and joy of life.

Therefore, we need to go for internal cleansing by look within in order to live in the now. We can create a feeling of loving, forgiveness, and gratitude, having a deep connection with nature, in order to create a huge space within to transcend ego and disconnect from thoughts of greed, lust, attachment, and endless desire in order to discover our true selves with the help of dynamic meditation practice as well as in the form of laughing, crying, dancing, swimming, and running. As we are internally cleansed, we can release negative emotional energy into the Universe because the Universe is a great empty place.

Negative Emotion into Positive Emotion

Negative emotion consists of fear, anger, jealousy, hatred etc. and it appears more frequently when we live in memory, projection, dream, imagination, and looking to others. If we waste time and energy on them, we end up losing our true selves. We are badly stuck in turmoil and inner noise. If we start living in the now by dissolving our thoughts of past and future, then we can observe that growth, positivity, love, and compassion are arising within us because we are able to discover our true selves, and there is no judgment and labeling but only possibilities, abundance, and opportunities around us.

As soon as we enter into this moment, we can be fully relaxed, which can free us from worry, anxiety, and fear. We begin to realize and experience who we really are, and we have the right answers to all the questions as soon as we let go of anger, anxiety, worry etc.

Create a Huge Space Within

Thoughts of anger, fear, sadness etc. interfere with this moment from memory, imagination, and the thinking mind, which creates a problem here right now. The final purpose of meditation is to create a huge space within to dissolve negativity, fear, anger, and darkness.

People who are not aware, they do not live in the now and bring negative emotion from the past into this moment. When you start living with them, their unawareness starts affecting you, but it depends upon you as well. You can accept or ignore their unawareness, but still you can heal them with compassion through creating a great space within the way Buddha did, the way Jesus Christ did, the way many more great teachers have done. They used to heal poor people with compassion by creating a huge space within through meditation practice to dissolve their negativity, hatred, fear, and darkness.

Presence of a Being

True presence is beyond thoughts, words, and actions. Life is an illusion, where most of the things are temporary in nature, but people who need material satisfaction end up in pain and suffering. Their true presence is affected because they are living in an illusionary world where they observe things as they are not.

People talk different from what they are because they have lost their real sense of being and live a dualistic pattern of life; therefore, they are not at peace, because they live with too much ego creating false ideas and close belief system around them, which takes away their honesty, truthfulness, and integrity. There is always evolution of consciousness from lower-level hatred, jealousy, anger, fear etc. to higher-level courage, truth, love, enlightenment etc. taking place in order to appear as a pure present state to understand the deeper meaning of life, but you have to live in the now. Those who are disoriented and lost in illusion end up in frustration because they are losing their true selves.

An atom is made up of 99.999 percent empty space, and that empty space is the pure present state. The present state is the fundamental state of existence, and it is the greatest truth of life that is available right now. Whatever we experience comes from this state. Everything originates from this state, like the Universe, galaxy, stars, and trees. The root of experience of any things, which we receive through sense, comes from this present state. It is the real state, where we can observe things as they really are, because our innermost being is silence in nature. This now is deeper in reality, but superficial reality is the body and mind. Whatever we experience through our senses— heat, cold, smell, touch, sensations of pain, light and darkness—we always experience in this moment.

When children are born, they do not have names and identification, but as they grow older, we label them as he is Sanjeev or John. Before labeling, the child was in a pure present state, but later on, his or her mind gets conditioned by living with family members, parents, and society, all of them help to develop false belief systems, rituals, and dogmas around the child.

Improve Quality of Life

You can discover who you really are when you take care of now. Many people waste time and energy by going into memory, flashback, and dream. They detach from the beautiful moments of life. Therefore, they cannot celebrate each and every moment of life, which finally decreases their inner capacity because they have no control over these moments. The only thing they have control over is the *now*.

Quality of life is based on the inner journey, when we are looking inside, but we are too often stuck with turmoil. People are busy in their daily lives, and they are looking for the outer world. They keep on losing touch with their beautiful inner lives because they are not able to know who they really are, which decreases the productivity of life. Awakening and transformation take place as a result of investigation and self-discovery when you go through major seatbacks in your life and try to know about your true self by asking insightful questions within. There is a major shift from pain to happiness, from anger to love, from fear to courage that takes place; negative emotions are converted into positive emotions, and you can observe that your quality of life has improved.

Practice meditation by sitting quietly for a few minutes every day and emptying all thoughts from your mind. You can light a candle and focus on the flames; watch and notice the flames, but do not concentrate on them, because concentration means force is exerted on the flames. Just be there and relax. See how beautiful the light is being emitted from the candle, but again, do not judge whether it is high- or low-intensity light; just witness it, and gradually there will be an emptying of all thoughts. It is meditation practice as well, and finally, you become the light.

Learn the Art of the Present Moment from Children

It is already proven that children are more mindful than adults. They are fresh in every moment in terms of experiencing. When you give them food, they taste, smell, and touch it by complete presence. They let go of everything very easily and move to the next level. Have you ever observed that they sleep very well without thinking? If they go to bed, they can sleep immediately without thinking; but when we go for sleep, we think about our jobs, families, past, future etc. and we cannot sleep properly, because our minds are highly conditioned and we can keep on thinking about useless thoughts without any reason.

Whenever children laugh, they keep on laughing without hesitation, and their laughing is full of joy and inner beauty, with deep presence in it, which is very powerful, because they have no judgment and labeling in them; but we cannot laugh properly, because we are badly stuck with inner noise and turmoil in the form of ego, and we are living into the past and future, which become obstacles to our laughing. Moreover, we are looking into others, and whenever we laugh, we can feel ego in them. We always label our thoughts by thinking that we are powerful and better than others, and again labeling and judgment are there, but children are one with everything and they have no judgment at all. Children attract more abundance in their lives because they live here right now, but we can keep on dwelling on the past because we live more with the conditioned mind than awareness.

Children are the best example of staying in this moment. Notice their activities in day-to-day life. You can observe that their presence in every moment is already there. They cherish every moment and all the blessings they have. When they face obstacles and challenges, they do not worry about it, because they do not know the meaning of challenges; moreover, they are totally present with mind, body, and soul and absorb whatever is around them. If they are around happy, positive people, they will also be healthy, innovative, and creative. Since their mind is so receptive that they can learn everything in this moment without thinking.

Children do not have much ego. They do not feel superior or inferior. If you ask a child to draw pictures—maybe different objects like telephones, shoes, scissors etc. you notice that they look at the pictures and start drawing very soon without objections; they never care about others. They are fully in this moment physically, mentally, and emotionally. They do not look at others to see what they are doing. Not only that, we can learn the trial-and-error method from children. It does not matter how many times they fail; they keep on trying by erasing and drawing many times until they achieve success.

Children are on autopilot in the activities of daily living. Children's minds are highly awakened and full of curiosity and innocence in nature; they live with awareness. When they are playing, they keep on playing for longer periods of time unless you disturb them, because their presence in every moment is immense and very powerful.

Watch Out for the Activities of a Kid

Observe children's smiles while playing with toys and swings. They know how to have fun. Sometimes they go for dancing, and we can observe their dancing movements. They are completely absorbed in every now because they are still fresh and they have more curiosity to know things. They go for an elephant or horse ride with a smiling face. They like to enjoy nature; they keep on asking questions about trees, sunshine, and sunset. They enjoy birds chirping. The main point is that children do every activity with watchfulness, not with the mind.

Every Activity Is a Teacher of Awareness

Whatever activity you do, when you do it with awareness, it brings total satisfaction. For example, when you prepare food with awareness, you are totally aware of every step while making rice in a pressure cooker. You can take rice and clean it with water before you put it in the rice cooker. This is the first step, and you are already there with awareness of the movement of each finger while cleaning. The next activity, you have to do is to put the water in the cooker, and then the last activity is to boil it on the stove, and finally it gets prepared. You can eat with sound taste because it is food of awareness.

To take your time in every step with the preparation of rice with awareness means to be present in each and every moment, whatever you are doing, which raises your productivity level. The taste and flavour of food must be very delicious, because whatever work you have done for preparation of it, you were totally present in every moment from your heart, not by the mind. You have already put awareness in every single step for making delicious food.

Another Meaning of Awareness is Alertness and Wakefulness

When you speak, you should speak with awareness, which means you do not have to speak what you do not want to speak. You are totally aware in each and every word while speaking, but relax and then you can speak with awareness. You can speak without awareness, but it does not make any sense, because you are not aware of each word, but it is wonderful if you fill the gap between two words. People can speak with space in deep awareness; if they are in a transcendental state already, whatever they speak, the words are divine with bliss.

When you walk, walk with awareness means you have to first heel strike, and then flat your feet, and the last step is to raise on your toes; these are the normal movement pattern in walking. If you are aware in all these movements, then your walking becomes bliss. This is our meditation practice. Awareness always flows through us, with no time or space.

Another example is eating an apple. We can go for eating an apple without awareness, but that does not bring any satisfaction at all. Take a bite and chew it, but go on watching. Let the watcher be there in every moment and then eating would be bliss. Awareness means you need to be an observer and keep on observing while eating an apple!

People keep on talking and doing other works while eating, which is not good. While eating if you are doing some other work, it means you are not aware every moment because you are not fully alert, conscious, and awake; you have already distracted your attention to something else, like talking. You need to be fully alert and awake in every activity whatsoever you are doing, whether you are driving a car or running.

Life Gives You Many Opportunities

When you closely observe every activity of daily living, you can learn it very easily. For example, while combing, you need to hold the comb with a light touch and comb with it, but be aware in every movement. While eating, if you are eating with a spoon, try to hold it with awareness means to be alert, awake, and conscious while bringing a spoon toward the mouth; otherwise you miss the mouth.

What happens when somebody hurts you? You get mad and sad because that person has insulted you—but the insult is no more an insult when you are aware. You may even smile. It does not hurt; it hurts only when you received it in unawareness. That person hurt you because he or she was manifesting his or her own suffering by insulting and hurting you, it does not mean that we have to hurt them back. Rather, we must forgive them. That is the real meaning of awareness.

Listening and Watching in Awareness

Listen to the chirping of the birds with no chirping and wandering of the mind inside. Look at the sun and feel the rising of awareness within you; you can feel that a ray of light has entered into your soul. The deeper your watchfulness becomes, the sharper your awareness becomes. Like your thought process, when one thought goes and another has not yet come, there is a gap, and you will have glimpses of no-mind. In that space, suddenly the sky becomes blue and clear and the sun is shining.

Do Not Lose Touch with the *Now*

Every moment is divine and productive. You can lose your true self when you lose touch with the now. Nothing exists beyond it, because this is all we have. We can feel dead if we do not live here and now. It does not matter how much power we have. Losing touch with the now makes us powerless.

Here is a great example. A child enjoyed his life with his mother when he held his mother's finger in a crowd for a painting competition as other children were enjoying. He always smiled, was happy, and had fun. It was really great, but I observed and noticed the same child after he lost touch with his mother's hand by mistake. What happened to him in the next moment? He became nervous and cried in pain; he threw all his toys and kept on searching and looking for his mother desperately. As soon as he found his mother again, he became okay. He enjoyed playing with his toys and had fun with the other tools again. What is this?

What we observed here was how happy he was as long as he held his mother's finger; he was enjoying every moment. But all of a sudden, when he lost touch with her, he started crying. He felt disappointed. So one moment may be sad, but the next moment may be happy. So just imagine when he was happy and came to a sad moment: he forgot everything about happiness completely and moved into the next moment of sad, so it is not good to disconnect with any moment of life, whether it is good or bad; experience them.

Accept every moment as it is and dive into them deeply with surrender; there you can find inner joy and real beauty of life. Let go of every moment no matter how beautiful or painful it is; move on to the next moment.

Each moment is different for experience, and it keeps on changing. As long as I lived in India, people used to talk about others, saying that they had enough land, money, property etc. They tried to boast about themselves and belittle others, but it is futile. What you have right now does matter; you do not need to talk about those things that you do not have right now. People often miss this now by talking about the past.

Practices in Daily Living

1. Let's say I am making breakfast for my friend. I am preparing a sandwich. I am cutting different vegetables with a knife in order to put the vegetables inside the bread. I would hold the knife with a light touch and start cutting the vegetables. Just imagine what would happen if I would be thinking about something else—may be about my wife, kids, or father—while cutting the vegetables. There are chances that I could cut my finger because I am thinking about something else in this moment, and it decreases my productivity level. On the other hand, if I am present in this moment, I can definitely make the sandwich better and more delicious because I am putting awareness in each and every step for preparation of it.

2. I have seen people slam the door while closing it. It happens when they are not living here right

now. It means they are thinking about something different while closing it, result in a loud sound. When we are present in this moment, if someone asks us to close the door, we just hold it with a light touch and pull it comfortably; no sound comes out, because we are mindful and relaxed in the now.

3. What happens when a doctor does an operation? If he is totally there mindfully, that is okay; but as soon as he moves into the past or future by thinking about his wife, kids etc. he is not able to focus on the operation, because past memory or thinking about the future is interfering with this moment. This leads to an unsuccessful operation because he was not in this moment while doing the operation. The more the doctor lives in the moment with mindfulness practice, the better the operation is because mindfulness raises productivity level.

4. It is the same as when you are in a traffic zone, where noises are coming from honked horns and people are crying and shouting on the street. When you are mindful and living in the now, it does not affect you at all because you are just focusing on awareness of breath. You are not judging any thoughts of noises, horns, but just watching and witnessing of them.

5. Eat meals with mindfulness and gratitude. Taste every morsel of food and enjoy the aroma, flavor, taste, and texture of your food.

6. Take soap, rinse with water, and finally, you can clean the dishes. You are focused on every activity of cleaning the dishes because you are

already there. But just imagine when you are there physically, but mentally you are thinking about fun, movie, work etc. Your attention goes somewhere else, and you cannot clean the dishes properly, may be you can drop few utensils; lack of mindfulness decreases productivity level.

7. You can notice sunlight, the ocean, mountain, rain, wind, tree, sight, and sound on your way to work while driving a car when you are in the now. You can enjoy with them, but never judge and label them; just witness of them. The more you are present in this moment, the better you will relax and celebrate each and every moment.

8. If I am sipping a cup of tea in this moment, I can enjoy the taste and flavor of tea. But what would happen if I am thinking about something else— maybe about my parents, kids etc. while sipping a cup of tea? I can burn my tongue because I am trying to bring the past into this moment, which is not possible, and finally it decreases my productivity level.

9. While driving, we are listening to the radio, talking on cell phone, text messaging, and combing our hair. The now gets lost in all these activities because while driving we are doing many things all together. We could meet with an accident because endless distractions and mind wanderings can take us away from being in the now.

In order to be fully in the moment, we must detach our beliefs, ideas, and opinions from everything; by this means we can become more aware and conscious of what we are actually experiencing in the now.

Difference Between Periphery and Center of Being

We can experience good or bad, positive or negative, but as soon as we reach at the center of being, everything is dissolved and there is nothing left over but pure awareness, which is beyond all kinds of experiences and it comes from thoughtless state where true being is there in the form of pure presence, which is called the present state, where all duality is dissolved and the innermost being is present in the form of true self; pain and misery are lost, and you are no more who you are. There is no self, and "I" is also dissolved; you become one with everything, and you are able to discover who you really are and get interconnected with heart, not with the mind. You are detached with all kinds of attached thoughts. You are beyond mind and body and remain in the silence state. You can observe invisible things while living at the center of being. In the center, you are deeply connected with the inner world; you are fully in this moment, with inner joy, happiness, and peace.

Unconditional love and deep connection with the Universe source energy is there, and you are fully eternal at the center of being, where time and space are already dissolved.

Mind is chattering and wandering at the periphery; you remain with mind, not with heart, where you are thinking about past and future and bringing them into this moment. There is deviation and distraction, with loss of awareness of breath, because past and future are taking control of now, and you are lost in delusion and get connected with the outer world. You are more physical because you live with words, actions, and thoughts. Your life is based on judgment and labeling.

The origin of true love is from the center, but fear, anger, hatred, negativity etc. arise from the periphery.

Relax into This Moment

As soon as you move into the next moment, be relaxed and let go of previous moment, whether it is a moment of pain or happiness, love or hatred; surrender in deep trust and love because each moment is new and fresh.

The right meaning of meditation is total surrender; fully relax into this moment the way existence wants you to be. Let go of thoughts of anger, fear, jealousy, hatred etc. Never be attached to any kind of thoughts of desire or prejudice; meditation is an act of deconditioning and deprogramming as well. There is nothing inside but the true presence of being, which is beyond all experiences in your life. This means we can have experiences good or bad, positive or negative, but we need to go beyond all these experiences in order to live now. Mind is full of distraction, disconnection, disturbance, disease, and deviation. As soon as you are free from all of these, you are fully in this now; this is the present state, where you are alert, awake, and watchful. This is also called the no-mind state, where truth descends.

We cannot relax into this moment, because we are burdened with unnecessary things and surrounded with beliefs, disbeliefs, dogmas, rituals, scriptures etc. All of these accumulate inside in the form of useless and unwanted thoughts that end up into cluttering of the mind. Therefore, we need to remove all unnecessary things and unburden ourselves in order to get relaxed. The more unburdened you are, the lighter you can feel, and only truth happens.

Each Moment Is Blissful

Each moment is new, fresh, and powerful, but never judge it, whether it is painful or beautiful; just witness and observe it.

I met one of the richest persons alive. He shared his intense pain because he was under a high-stress level. He is seventy years old now, and he spent forty years of life in order to be rich; now he is rich, but still he is in deep pain, as he complains that he wasted forty years of beautiful moments of life to deal with employees. He struggled hard in order to become rich, but he is now repentant that he did not celebrate each and every moment of life; rather, he suffered in pain because he had connected with many illusionary and useless thoughts of material things based on a give-and-take relationship with his conditioned mind.

His main question was, how could he bring back millions of the beautiful moments of life that he already wasted? But he cannot bring them back, even if he wants to. He is helpless and lived in the outer world to know life with the mind; he did not live in the inner world. Moreover, he lost his true self in order to deal with many employees, businesses etc. so there is no point to go back, because those moments are already gone. His life is miserable because he did not enjoy his life so far. His next problem is that he cannot sit in silence, because he used to deal everything with conditioned mind; he developed the habit of doing it, which means he cannot live in peace and inner joy. He has tried living in the now several times, but he could not because his mind is chattering and wandering and never lets him sit in silence. He is getting more miserable day by day; he needs compassion and love.

He can live in the now and try to get disconnected from past moments by letting go of the past, attachment, desire, fear etc. He needs to get connected more with nature in order to dissolve his conditioned mind and reconnect with focus on the awareness of breath if the past is taking control of him in this moment. He needs to decondition and deprogram his mind.

Does Light Dispel Darkness?

As soon as you bring light in, darkness is no more. Light and darkness are opposites, but you need to go beyond that. The only thing that dispels hate is to bring love in. Love is light, and darkness is hate. But if you are living with light within, then you are radiating brightness around yourself, but darkness is also within you. Both have to exist in the human life.

Darkness is in the form of thoughts of memory, illusion, dream, flashback, imagination, goal, ambition, projection, and so forth, but light is always here right now.

Darkness itself is a negative state of mind; it has no existence. It always wants to live in negative situations and people because it does not exist. So how can you live with it if it does not exist anymore? As soon as you bring light in, darkness is gone completely. But never fight with darkness; when you fight with it, it would persist more, so just bring light in—that is all you need do. Darkness is the absence of light.

There are two kinds of darkness; one is positive, and the other one is negative.

Positive darkness creates the origin of light. I suffered in intense pain, but I know that without darkness, light was not possible. I encountered many of the worst moments of my life to get the light, and ultimately I got it. If I had not faced those worst moments in my life, I would not have evolved and met with growth and development. That darkness was an immense blessing for me. Therefore, darkness creates the origin of light.

Life is not possible without darkness because it opens many opportunities and attracts abundance in your life, but people do not observe it closely; therefore, they are one step away from it. Without it no rays of hope can come; without it no light is possible; without it no growth and development is possible. It is a blessing in disguise, a diamond in coal. So never try to get away from it.

It does not matter how many dark moments you face; always try to follow the right path, be authentic, honest, and truthful, and try to bring light in. Light has to come, and it will come. It is already there, but you are lost in the illusion of thoughts of mind. It will always come at the last moment, but you must create a great trust within no matter what happens. If you want to create a great spark in the world, then never lose the darkness; but dissolve all negativity and dark moments of life by living into this moment, and then nothing wrong ever happens.

Never be afraid of darkness. If you face failures and are unsuccessful, do not stop it; stick with your goal. Whatever field you have, whether it is a career, relationship, business, or something else, do not worry but keep moving on like a lion. Face hundreds of thousands of failures. Continued failing does not make you worry, because light is going to come at the end. If it does not come, then it shows that either you are not true to yourself or you have done wrong with others; there is always a brighter luminous light waiting for you, and you will receive it. It is the law of nature.

The other kind of darkness is negative darkness, one that is full of turmoil and chaos. It happens when people are not honest and truthful; they try to deceive and hurt others because they are looking in others and are lost in dream, memory, and the illusion of thoughts of the past and future. Finally, they are creating negative darkness, and their life is based on judgment.

As soon as Buddha had gone for meditation, he was attacked by the demon named Mara, but basically it was not the demon that attacked. It was his own destructive capacity in the form of useless and illusionary thoughts of anger, fear etc. which put him in the past and future with darkness that created a disturbance in his meditation practice. He was not scared at all; he touched the ground and said that earth exists into this moment, not the thoughts. This is the truth, and he witnessed it. As soon as he touched the earth, all useless and illusionary thoughts went away. Thoughts do appear and disappear.

Observation of Life Situations

I have seen people who experienced trauma and tragedy a long time ago in the form of an accident. It is really bad that they had tragedy, but it is worst that they dwelled upon it for a long period of time, because when you dwell upon tragedy, it means you are living in memory and flashback, and we cannot change the past at all. How can you bring the past into this moment? It is impossible because the past is last, and the present has started. But still we cry for a few moments, which is normal because we release our stuck energy in the form of tears; we feel sorry for that person.

When we cry for longer periods of time by just thinking in flashback and memory, it leads to pain and suffering because we are trying to control the past by living here now, which is not possible. It is just a waste of time and energy. It leads to disease, heart attack, psychiatric illness etc. Therefore, it is better to forget and let go of the thoughts of the past and keep moving to the next moment.

One Candle can Light Thousands of Candles

It is absolutely right that a single candle can light thousands of candles, but the light of a single candle is not diminished. Light cannot be diminished by spreading the light for others. The more you share true knowledge with others, the more you learn, grow, and evolve, which is wisdom. It means you are enhancing your knowledge by others' knowledge, and your knowledge cannot be diminished by sharing it—sharing it with the right person is needed. Buddha used to teach and share about meditation practice, and this knowledge spread all over the world.

We try to hide the truth from others because we are limited by ego. Ego can limit and close our minds; with closed minds, we do not want to share knowledge with others. We try to keep it within ourselves, but sooner or later this knowledge is no more, so we lose everything we had before. People are not ready to listen, accept, and share with others because they are limited by their own belief systems, which is really bad.

What we observe here is that when a candle was not lit, it was in the past and it had no value; but as soon as we light a single candle, it shows that this moment has started entering now. Finally, when a single candle has spread the light to other candles, it has made us aware that the whole power of the Universe is already within us, but we need to live right now.

Another Example of a Life Situation

A woman looks beautiful in one moment, but when you start living with her, she looks ugly in the next moment, so it does not matter how beautiful or ugly she is. What does matter is how good she is at heart. All people are good at heart, but we judge them on the basis of outer looks, which is not good. Every person is beautiful but judgment can take you into the past or future.

Discover Your True Self

We are here for growth and development, and there is no value of life if we do not want to evolve. We have tremendous potential within, but we may never know it, because we are living in an illusive world where everything is superficial and people are busy in the illusions; therefore, they cannot go inside and look within in order to know true self, who they really are. What is the purpose of life? Why are we here? Who am I? How can we get connected with the Universe in order to know our true selves? These kinds of deep, insightful questions arise within us when we have the right intention to know the truth because we want to see the things as they really are.

We are lost in the outside world, where we are more connected and attached with thoughts of the material world of the past and the future; moreover, we are living in a conditional life based on a give-and-take relationship, which finally creates pain and suffering in our lives; therefore, we cannot discover our true hidden potential as long as we are living in the outer world. We can know our potential as soon as we look within in order to reach at the center of being by answering deep, insightful questions, but the outer world is temporary and attractive, and when we waste energy and time with the outer world, we are not able to discover our higher selves. The more we live right now, creating a space within with the help of meditation and deep connection with nature, then we can know our hidden potential and move from periphery to the center of being by dissolving ego.

Most people are badly stuck with ego; they think that they know everything, but they do not know it, because it is illusion. Ego can keep a person on the periphery; therefore, we need to dissolve it by living in the now, and then we can move to the center of being and answer all questions. Thus, we can discover our true potential. Stay connected with water, rocks, mountains, and trees, which can refresh, rejuvenate, and relax our lives into this moment because it dissolves the past experiences and bring inner joy and peace.

Heavy Food Is Distraction

Most of the food is heavy like rice, potato etc. whosoever eat them gets too much distracted, which makes them lazy; they may go on thinking about the past and the future. Moreover, these are not nature-connecting foods, and you cannot live in this moment with them; therefore, meditation is needed in order to focus on the awareness of breath.

On the other hand, if you take grapes, fruits, juices, vegetables, herbs, shrubs etc. your distraction level gets diminished because you are connected more with nature like water, air, sunrays etc. This is very light food, and it puts you more into this moment by disconnecting with the past and the future. This food would sharp your wisdom also and improve your productivity by raising your energy level. This kind of food is high vibration-energy food in nature, and it can absorb nature completely. It protects you from any disease by creating a strong immunity system; it helps you to develop a few powerful focused thoughts that we need.

Think about those people who eat lots of meats of different kinds in the form of low-vibration energy foods. They create many distractions because such food is heavy in nature and animal products as well; true nature is not there, but only dead life is present. Therefore, it might affect their creativity and innovation. Their productivity level goes down and they cannot sharp their skills, and they can live more in the past and the future. They get thoughts of diseases, thoughts of violence etc. They are not able to focus into this moment. It affects their thought pattern system, and it is very difficult to overcome inner chaos and turmoil within themselves!

Knowledge Versus Wisdom

People keep on collecting false knowledge by reading many books, scriptures, religious articles etc. and they develop too much ego because they are not creating something new; moreover, they depend on others' knowledge. This means they are losing the power of creation. Finally, they will lose their true selves and live in the past and future. Not only that, they are putting too much pressure and effort into learning which is not good because they are not aware about real knowledge.

Real knowledge or wisdom is significant when it grows within with effortless effort, not forced upon or by working hard. Real knowledge is always available in nature, but you need to have a deep connection with it. It is a never-ending process, gained through learning, sharing, and practical application through knowing of true self, which is based on experience, discovery, and self-realization. It is connected through the power of creation. It is never gained through reading religious books, scriptures etc. These create too much ego and obstacles on the path of growth and development because it is written by others and people just follow them without deep understanding, which creates a false belief system and closes our minds because it stops our curiosity to ask deep, insightful questions. Wisdom is already available in us, but we need to look within, investigate, and explore it. It comes by living in the now!

There is nothing to learn. You have to be ready to unlearn! You already know too much, and all that you know is false; think of unlearning. That is the beginning of wisdom, but again, basic knowledge is required; we must learn how to eat food and live a good ordinary life with basic things like food, shelter, and clothing. Everything should be in balance.

When I was in school, I read very few books, just those that were needed as per the syllabus. The instructors used to teach me to remember, memorize, and cram the words. They did not teach me beyond books, and finally, they conditioned and programmed my brain to go for limited knowledge; this affected my creativity, exploration, and discovery. Later on, I noticed that my growth and development had already stopped because I did not go beyond books. I could be deeply connected with existence only when I could empty my mind of all kinds of thoughts; cramming, memorizing, and reading filled me up with too many thoughts, which affected my wisdom, and later on, I realized that I had lost the power of creation. The instructors used to teach me about fullness but not emptiness.

Wisdom is to go beyond knowledge, and it happens when you try to expand knowledge, which means thinking beyond your thoughts, full of imagination, and creativity. But they taught me to move into the future and past, and finally my inner capacity decreased. Repression started taking place, and I tried to fight it with my mind by repeating the same thoughts again and again, as it happens in the beginning of meditation.

True knowledge Happens Within You

The right meaning of true knowledge or wisdom is to empty yourself of all useless and purposeless thoughts of dream, imagination, planning, goal, success, failure etc. in the process of unlearning. The true origin of wisdom is from thoughtless space within, when the mind becomes hollow, absolutely empty, pure, uncontaminated, unpolluted, and fresh; but be alert, aware, awake, and conscious—just like a newborn child who has no knowledge because he or she is ignorant.

Focus Your Energy

The sun is very powerful. Since it is not focused on a single object, it is less powerful. If it starts focusing on a single object, that object would catch fire. Our lives are similar. We know that we have a tremendous amount of power, but if we are not focused and are dispersing our energy into different activities, we cannot be successful. In order to focus while doing any activity, we have to live in the now.

When we center our energy, it creates great power. Centering is just gathering our energy at one point and paying full attention to it. Once we gather energy at one point, that point generates tremendous power. This is called the point of power. The point of power is always in the now. It always takes place when we have focused and refocused our energy. It is so powerful that it can change our lives completely. If we are not centering our energy, we remain unfocused; our energy would be spread out, and it would be wasted.

There is a difference between concentration and meditation. Concentration is to focus on a single object and bring total energy into this moment. We can judge our thoughts, whether something is good or bad, so gradually we are conditioning our mind; but meditation means dropping all barriers and deconditioning our minds, just objectively observing and witnessing of our thoughts. Concentration means too much effort and force within the programmed mind end up living in the past and future, which leads to suffering. But meditation means effortless effort and relaxation into this moment, which leads to inner joy and peace.

Meditation is inner discovery, but it is not the goal. Stop running here and there but try to discover and rediscover higher self within you. A goal exists in the future because you have a dream and are looking for something to happen, but meditation is fully in this moment. When the mind is no longer moves toward the past and future, you have to live in the now. Everything is dissolved. Suddenly you are flooded with light, joy, and peace; you are blessed. Those who taste the power of meditation cannot turn back, because it is something mysterious and secret and it comes only to those who open their hearts, not minds.

Another meaning of meditation is to surrender. Surrender means being free from ego and positivity takes place because you are becoming harmonious and one with existence.

Benefit of the Present Moment

We can deeply connect with the Universe and become one with everything. In deep presence, the boundary between objects and us is lost. When we are here in the now without thinking, it means we are one. A higher and powerful dimension opens—that dimension is awareness. Awareness means to be in the moment totally with alertness and watchfulness; past and future have no control in this moment. Everything stops, and we are synchronized and aligned with the frequency of the Universe. Only the present is here.

When you go to the park, do not think about the names and colors of flowers, but think about how beautiful they are and enjoy their fragrance by observation and watchfulness as a whole. There is nothing in your mind that you are thinking, but you have to witness the flower.

CHAPTER 2

Mind Is Suffering

Mind is a chattering and wandering box. Another meaning of mind is to live in the past and the future, full of thoughts of yesterday and tomorrow. Mind means tension, worry, anxiety, imagination, projection, doubt, confusion, chaos, and turmoil; therefore, mind cannot let you live in peace, because mind is deceptive, dual, and cunning in nature. It is full of illusionary and unproductive thoughts and creates misery because it disconnects with this beautiful moment. We have to notice, observe, and witness of thoughts, but never try to label and judge them at all, whether they are positive or negative, right or wrong, good or bad, in order to live in the now; then you can dissolve and decondition your mind.

The people who live with mind cannot live with awareness, because mind means thinking. Another property of mind is judgment and labeling. For example, when they look at the trees, they say leaves are green (yellow when the leaves are dried up); they cannot enjoy the beauty of leaves as a whole, because they are judging them, but as soon as they live with awareness, their minds dissolve into no-minds. They just watch, witness, and observe the leaves as they really are, without any judgment, and they drop the mind.

Whatever is happening around you is deeply rooted in the mind. Mind means time, but this present moment can transcend time and space as well. Time consists of two tenses, the past and the future. The mind has no present, only the past and the future. You are not the mind; you are beyond mind. We suffer because we condition and identify our minds. We need to drop our minds and suffer less by just witnessing and observation of the thoughts; do not identify with any of them, whether they are positive or negative, this or that. It is about witnessing, and in that witnessing, all questions and answers dissolve. The mind dissolves. Only silence remains with pure awareness.

Mind is an obstacle on the path of meditation. Mind means the past, and the past is dead, already gone. You can cut yourself off from the mind in order to live now and achieve the no-mind state; then you can answer thousands of questions without knowing. Mind knows only about knowledge that is full of scriptures, books etc. which is dangerous because it makes you sick and dead again and takes you into the past and the future.

Pain, suffering, and unhappiness come from judgment and labeling of mind. All negativity is caused by thinking too much, because the mind is full of negative thoughts; tension, stress, and worry—all forms of fear—are caused by not living in the now. Guilt, regret, resentment, sadness, bitterness, negativity, and darkness are present when we dwell on the past and future. Through the mind there is misery, anxiety, pain, suffering, worry, and death; but through meditation there is happiness, bliss, inner joy, peace etc.

We must keep on dropping the whole past and future without any choice; then misery disappears.

Desire Creates Pain and Suffering

As we know, pain arises when we identify and condition our mind. Mind is the root cause of suffering, and desire is part of mind.

Craving, greed, lust, desire etc. create suffering and pain. They may bring temporary satisfaction, but they create misery in the long run. All kinds of cravings come from within us when we have endless desires and live with mind. Most people have too many desires. They need big houses, many cars etc. and in order to fulfill their desires, they end up in pain and suffering because they disperse their energy level into different material activities in order to satisfy themselves, but as soon as one desire is satisfied, the next desire comes out, and they are busy and occupied in those desires; they lose their true selves and are not able to discover who they really are, because they have lost a great amount of time and energy. A question arises: How can you live happily? You cannot live happily with peace, inner joy, and abundance when you have endless desires, because they create greed, lust, and craving and block your happiness.

Mind is thought and thought is mind. As soon as we provide a gap or space between two thoughts, less suffering takes place because this space is the pure present state and available in this moment; it dissolves all pain, misery, hatred, lie, and fear.

As soon as you enter this moment, be relaxed and let go of the past, let go of memory, and let go of flashback. You have the right answers of all the questions by dissolving all negativity; your inner presence then gets stronger and sharper, and you can listen to inner guidance. Whenever you feel any kind of negative emotion, just take a deep breath and relax.

Pain, suffering, negativity, and darkness are deeply rooted in time, but positivity is always in this moment. All negativity is caused by an accumulation of negative-thought emotion energy and denial of this moment. Discomfort, anxiety, tension, stress, worry, fear, guilt, regret, resentment, and pain are all the result of living in mind or time!

End of Suffering

All things in the Universe are temporary and impermanent in nature; all things keep on changing. We are born, grow, and die. Matter changes into atoms, and atoms change into molecules; there is continuous evolution taking place, and we have deep curiosity to know the answer of all questions. Who am I? What is the purpose of life, and why are we here?

We know that as long as we have life, we have to suffer, but some of us suffer less while others suffer more, depending upon how we live! Most people suffer in great pain because they have wrong intentions, poor thoughts, and ill feelings and words, which bring suffering and pain whether they live consciously or unconsciously. The more you are attached, the more you suffer. Most of us create a duality pattern of life, and therefore, we suffer more. We suffer because we are not ready to accept the changes. The more we live with awareness, the less we suffer, because the now dissolves our mind.

As we know, every moment is new and fresh, and as soon we enter here and now, the past gets dissolved. Thoughts of fear, hatred, jealousy, negativity etc. come into this moment from the past and make us suffer more. A question comes: How can we get rid of them, and what is the root cause of such useless thoughts? Mind creates thoughts of greed, desire, lust etc. and it disconnects us from our true selves. These thoughts come when we start labeling and judging our thoughts with mind, but as soon as we live with meditation practice by focus on the awareness of breath, it reduces our suffering and we can live more with a deep connection with water, air, rock etc. in order to dissolve our minds.

Success and failure, life and death, pain and happiness come and go away. It cannot be stagnant and permanent with us, because each moment is different, but we are trying to find happiness in every moment through clinging and attachment that is not possible; suffering and pain follow in our lives because we try to cling to our attachments and desires. Nothing can be permanent, and the whole problem comes out when we want happiness every moment. Whatever comes, accept it with silence and gratitude.

Mind creates problems and traps us in chaos and turmoil. It makes us unpleasant and unhappy. It is very difficult for us to be free from it. But when we live in the now, we can be free from the mind. Pain, conflict, resistance, and suffering come from living in the past and future, which blocks our happiness because we are more connected with mind. As soon as we start living in the now, we can be free from the conditioning and identification of mind.

The more we are present in this moment, the sharper our experiences will be. When we suffer, there is immense power in it, but some people are closed-minded and they cannot experience that power; we need to be honest and truthful, and then we can know and experience that power. When I look back, I realize that if great tragedy had not happened, I would not be here on this path and sharing what I have learned, experienced, and realized. Again, everything happens for a good reason; therefore, create a huge amount of trust within yourself, and then everything will fall into the right place. This shift is so valuable in your life because it makes you aware that whatever happened with you a long time ago was inevitable. It had happened to show you the path of wisdom in order to discover your true great potential, which comes through experience. We must not dwell on the memory, flashback, and past, but try to learn from past experiences and move forward, no matter how painful they are.

There is a great lesson behind any experience. Next time when you are going to take any action or decision, be fully conscious, aware, alert, and attentive so that you do not repeat the same kind of mistakes again. You can investigate the causes of past mistakes into this moment, which helps you to grow, move to the next level, discover hidden potential, and sharpen your decision-making skills.

Our mind is full of desires, clinging, attachments, and longings. Mind is the root of all misery, which takes the form of ambition, desire, goal etc. Try to come out of mind and maintain a distance between you and mind; become a witness and watcher, and then slowly the mind will get dissolved. Mind is ego; as you dissolve mind, ego dissolves itself as well; then you can experience truth and discover who you really are.

The property of mind is to take you into the past; courage is to live into this moment, but again, mind tries to cling to the past. Whatever we do in day-to-day life is stored in memory, flashback, and experience in the form of the past. It is better to dissolve our minds by having a deep connection with water, rocks, mountains, and nature. These connect us with existence and release all memory and experience that you have stored for a long time.

In order to drop the past, we have to unlearn what we have learned; we must get rid of false knowledge that we accumulated through reading books, articles, scriptures etc. True courage is to move from the known into the unknown and become a child again, which means to live in the no-mind state, full of curiosity and innocence, in order to live with awareness. People think that they have courage for climbing mountains and taking risk for their businesses, but that is not real courage. They are looking outside and living in the past and future. Real courage is when we have to look within and live into this moment, with complete disappearance of mind in the form of past and future in order to end suffering.

Zen practice involves sitting and doing nothing. Their whole life is watchfulness and observation of thought, and they flow with existence without mind or any kind of judgment, with no attachment and no clinging. They totally live into this moment and overflow with joy. They can share joy, inner peace, and the beauty of life. They radiate truth silently without any judgment. They are really blessed and gifted with nature.

Most Zen practitioners are mystics; mystics are those who know the truth well. You can feel certain powerful energy and vibes flowing around them. Words are meaningless. They are totally absolute and empty. It seems that something has happened around them, and they gradually entered into the no-mind state with joy, bliss, beauty, and grace, blessed with nature. They go deeper and deeper into the state of aloneness in order to find their center of being, where eternal bliss prevails. They go beyond the experience of emptiness to where there is nothing to experience; only consciousness is there. There is no subject, no object, and no content; they are just there as observers and watchers.

CHAPTER 3

Thoughts Are Things

Only right and focused thoughts can discover who we really are because they travel. Words and actions are secondary. Words are just a way to convey messages; words are a reflection of our thoughts, and thoughts are a reflection of our feelings and intentions, but action is based on both of these! We are pure thought energy, which can discover the true essence of our innermost being.

Thoughts are impermanent, unreal, and momentary. Most of them are useless, illusionary, and futile. The real problem is when we identify and condition our thoughts but let them be as they are. They are like clouds that appear and disappear in the sky, but still the sky exists clearly, so let thoughts appear and disappear. We still live with the pure awareness of being, which means we need to witness of thoughts; our whole life is witnessing of thoughts. We can pay attention to the little gap between two thoughts and get a glimpse of the pure awareness to live in the now.

Mind is always chattering and wandering. If you are busy in chattering, your whole energy goes on thinking because every thought needs energy; finally, dissipation of energy takes place because of useless thoughts. As we know, the mind is full of thoughts like a cloud in the sky, and you cannot observe the sky clearly because the clouds cover it up. If you are wasting your energy for useless thoughts, then how can you bring more energy for the few powerful, focused thoughts that come from emptiness?

Only an Empty Mind Can Develop Focused Thoughts

Powerful thoughts are present at the center of being, but useless thoughts are present at the circumference; therefore, if you are chattering, it means your outer thoughts are active. They stop you from moving into the center of being, which results in separation of the true being and creates delusion because you are badly stuck in noises. You cannot observe the actual thoughts, which are already inside. You can observe things clearly as they really are only with an empty mind when you look within to move to the center of being in order to focus on real thoughts, but you are living outside.

Empty your mind and be like water, which is formless, shapeless, powerful, and abundant in nature. Water only flows through us if there are not any obstacles, but it is always empty. You can observe the transparent water from one side to another side. Our minds must be like water, which can see things clearly from one side to another side without any judgment, conditioning, and labeling; only then you can realize that how much your decision-making and reasoning skills have sharpened.

You can experience this in your daily life. Think of the number of thoughts you have in a day. On the next day, investigate and you'll find that 99.99 percent of your thoughts of yesterday were useless. But each thought is powerful, whether it is positive or negative, good or bad. If you have negative thoughts, they are equally powerful because they bring negativity into your life. For example, when you have a thought of fear, you can attract a similar situation in your life in the form of fear of losing your job, failing an examination, or messing up any project because like attracts like and each thought has a frequency and energy that vibrates at the highest level, so whatever you think that will manifest in your life, but it depends on the intensity and productivity of your thoughts as well.

If you have thoughts of hatred, you are going to attract a thought of enmity. Your thoughts must be consistent and powerful, with high intensity and focused as well; then you are going to attract what you think but there is another condition that applies. If you have created any weak thoughts—which are full of doubts—and confusions, that creates self-resistance and obstacles within, then you are not going to attract those thoughts into your life that you wanted because they are weak, inconsistent, and unproductive in nature. Again, like attracts like, which means you should avoid thoughts that are not powerful, productive, and useful; in order to attract what you want, you must have useful, productive, and powerful thoughts with high momentum, and they will bring everything into your life.

We attract people of the same frequency as we have. People who are at a lower frequency are dispelled in nature because their frequencies are not synchronized and aligned with a higher frequency. This means that true reflection always happens with people of the same frequency.

What we see, hear, and observe is based on what we perceive around us because we are truthful and honest and have clarity, which means that we are one with everything; but whenever we are not able to observe and hear things clearly and properly, it means we are full of useless and illusionary thoughts of confusion and doubt, and we create obstacles within. We are not able to see and perceive things clearly as they really are, because we are not one with everything; true reflection cannot happen in this moment. It is just like water: when it is transparent, you can observe things clearly from both sides, but when it is dirty, you cannot see the water from both sides, because it is covered by dirty particles. The same thing happens with our thoughts. If we have clear thoughts, free from attachment, desire, ego, and mind, definitely they would manifest in our lives sooner or later; but when we have confused thoughts, what we want may not manifest itself. Therefore, clear your thought process to manifest the right things in your life.

We often encounter negative thoughts—thoughts of fear, thoughts of worry, thoughts of pain, thoughts of suffering. Can we live without these thoughts? We cannot live without them. We know that these thoughts come and go. Generally they come from an unknown and empty space, but we have to witness and observe them as long as we do not judge and label them; as soon as we judge them, we can move into the past or future. Sometimes thoughts can take control of us, or we can choose to control them; it depends on how we live. As long as we live in the now, thoughts cannot control us, so it is better to be in this moment and observe the thoughts as they really are.

Cancer is not a deadly disease; it is bundles of negative thought energy inside that come from low-vibration food, negative environments, conditioning of our thoughts, and living with negative people. For example, when we eat meat, which is a low-vibration negative-energy food, it brings temporary satisfaction, but later on it affects our thought patterns. Maybe we could have more violent and destructive thoughts with distraction and deviation. Gradually such negative-thought energy accumulates inside and causes cancer and illness; we are not able to focus on work, because our minds start chattering and wandering more because of too many thoughts of past and future interfering with the now. Each thought has energy and frequency, which travels to the Universe; it attracts and brings same things into our lives because like attracts like, and therefore, when we create negative thought energy with the help of low-vibration foods, we attract same thing into our lives, maybe in the form of cancer. It is better to develop a few powerful, focused thoughts by meditation than to have many useless thoughts of negative energy without meditation.

Every thought occupies the same space, whether it is positive or negative, we have to accept whatever is there. It does not matter whether you are successful or a failure. We must consider life as a wholeness and completeness. Many teachers share their thoughts about the power of positive thinking, success, positive mental attitude, goal, dream, ambition etc. but they do not share their thoughts about the power of negative thinking, failure, darkness, negativity etc. Either they do not know about this or they have not experienced it in their lives; rather, they teach you to live in the future by showing a dream, ambition, and goal. My question is, why can't they talk about the power of negative thinking, failure, and living in the now?

Life is to know wholeness and completeness, which means knowing both sides of life, and then it is complete. Can electricity flow only through positive poles? No, it cannot flow at all with only positive poles; both poles are required. The negative pole is equally important. Can we get light without darkness? No, both things are required in order to exist. Light cannot exist without darkness. In the same way, we can get real peace only by overcoming chaos and inner turmoil within. Everything is needed. Nature balances everything in our lives. Teaching about one part of life is a half truth, and a half truth is more dangerous than a single lie. We must know about both sides of a coin, if we have thoughts of success that occupy the same space as thoughts of failure. Deep understanding is needed.

We must accept every moment of life, whether it is good or bad, painful or happy, and we must enjoy both of them in order to be self-realized and fulfillment! Never try to escape from the negativity and darkness of your life, because this is also a beautiful moment. The taste and flavour of negativity is necessary because life must be understood as a whole, then it is complete for liberation and evolution, which makes you powerful and strong.

We waste time and energy in judging and labeling of thoughts because we have collected too many useless thoughts. Only an empty mind can create focused thoughts that are already hidden in nothingness or awareness.

Every thought needs energy, and we waste our energy for useless thoughts. Real thoughts come from emptiness. If we waste all our energy in useless thoughts, then there is no energy left for the powerful thoughts that are already hidden in emptiness.

How can you know about true self when you are full of thoughts? You cannot, because many thoughts take you away from true self. As soon as you look within, then you can discover who you really are. In order to live with nothingness, we have to go beyond mind, which means we must live with awareness, which happens when we disconnect from thoughts of past and future by bringing awareness of breath at the top of the nostrils, which helps you to create nothingness to know the true potential thoughts.

The Thoughtless State

The thoughtless state is a neutral, nonjudgmental, and nonreactive state that does not attach to any thoughts of sadness, hatred etc. The whole Universe is between positivity and negativity, and the thoughtless state arises between the two.

You can observe invisible things when you are in the thoughtless state during meditation, and watching invisible things creates a miracle. You can reach toward a higher power as soon as you create nothingness, which is the final objective of meditation, equal to knowing of a higher power. Nothingness is a state of pure awareness, which does not care whether something is good or bad, positive or negative, because it is nonjudgmental; it takes care as a whole! Light and darkness are within us, but we can observe only darkness; we cannot observe the light, because it is hidden within us, and we cannot see it, because we are not doing meditation. As soon as we start living in the now, we can observe the light that is already there.

Too many thoughts create haziness and darkness within us because we are living in delusion, where we can observe things around us as they are not. These useless thoughts come from the past and the future. The main thought of this moment is already hidden in now, but you are lost because you do not know it; as soon as you practice living in the now, then you can know the main thoughts of productivity.

I am sharing words from the space between two thoughts with effortless effort in this moment, and words just flow because this space is the pure, thoughtless space where every word is blissful and divine. It is taking place because beautiful thoughts pop into our minds from unknown and empty spaces, and you can also notice that all my words are fully aware, which means I share what needs to be shared, but I do not share which is not required.

As we know, some people are not sharing right words, because they live in the past and future by thinking about something else in this moment. They keep on sharing without knowing the proper meaning of their words because they share from a fullness of thoughts, not from emptiness; therefore, their words are not powerful. Again, you need to focus on the awareness of breath wherever you are.

"In the center, you are true being, a vast space, silent, and blissful."-Sanjeev Kumar

CHAPTER 4

Focus on the Breath

We must focus on awareness of the breath wherever we are, whether we are in school or at work. If you are playing football with your friends, you can keep on playing football, but still bring the sensation of awareness of the breath at the top of the nostrils. Relax into this moment with effortless effort, and do nothing; just breathe in and breathe out, and let the thoughts come in and go away. Just witness and observe them; never judge any kind of thought, but try to develop the sensation of awareness of the breath at the top of the nostrils, which is our practice. Gradually you can observe that you become one with the breath. It does not matter how many times you disconnect with breath but keep coming back on the breath is our practice.

We must practice this in all activities of daily living. As we know, mind is full of thoughts, and it never lets you live into this moment, because mind means past. Maybe you could disconnect with this moment while you are under control of mind and there are thoughts of fear, anger, hatred etc. interfering with this moment. Again, mind means future in the form of ambition, projection, and imagination, but just bring your awareness back to the breath and let go of thoughts of fear, anger etc. No matter how beautiful thoughts may be—they could be thoughts of your children, parents etc.—just witness them; never label and judge any kind of thoughts, whether they are positive or negative, and gradually you will observe that you are living into this moment, and the past and the future do not affect you at all, because you can practice bringing the sensation of breath at the top of the nostrils.

Overcome Obstacles

Always take a relaxed breath whenever you are experiencing anxiety, worry, stress, and fear. Most of the obstacles created by living in memory, imagination, projection, dream etc. because we are thinking too much about what would, could, and should have happened.

Power of Awareness of Breath

Breath is a life-force energy that exists in the now. Breathing is the process by which we get connected to existence. This is the ultimate bliss. Without it we are not anymore, but a question arises: How many people are aware of breath?

A few years back, when I was not transformed I never knew about the awareness of breath. As soon as I start living in the now, I came to know about it. Life and death are just two expressions of the same energy of self, because energy is neither created nor lost but it changes from one form to another form. When we are born we have breath, and when we die we lose breath; therefore, breath is life-force energy. It connects us between life and death.

If you are aware of breath every time you breathe, you are living in the now; but if you are not aware of it, you move into a different dimension, maybe in the past or future.

Meditation is simply feeling the sensation of breath. I can challenge that those who suffer from depression, anxiety disorder etc. they can get rid of all such kinds of diseases by being aware of breath daily for at least six months. They will begin to feel bliss and inner joy. Breath has transformed millions of lives. It dissolves negativity and darkness and overcomes fear.

If tension, anxiety, and worry happen to you, do not move into the future but just bring your awareness of the breath at the top of the nostrils and connect with the divine moment, because it only exists here and now. If you are not aware of breath, you can move into memories, flashbacks, and dreams again.

It is better to dissolve our minds to live here right now. Breath transcends ego, and it breaks you free from your mind through deconditioning. Finally, it creates a great space within.

Wherever you are, just be aware of your breath. Even when you go to bed for sleep, just focus on the awareness of breath before sleeping, and then your sleep will be bliss. Breath connects with existence and clears and dissolves useless thoughts. Nature-loving people are pure because they keep on taking in fresh oxygenated air, which can dissolve unwanted and useless thoughts.

Most people who live in urban surroundings are not happy because they put conditioning on everything based on a give-and-take relationship; they live with mind, not with heart, and they cannot breathe fresh oxygenated air, because there is too much pollution by cars, vehicles, close buildings, and many other things that can block fresh air. On the other hand, when you go to rural surroundings, the people live a different kind of life. They are more connected with fresh nature and take in fresh oxygenated air, which can dissolve their minds so they can live in the now and be free from illusionary thoughts; therefore, they are honest and truthful and attract abundance and joy in their lives.

CHAPTER 5

Ego and Ways to Transcend It

Ego is lower self, not true self. We can feel superior, inferior, powerful, strong, and dominant because of too much ego. The whole world is full of conflict, chaos, and suffering because of it. Self-esteem, self-respect, and self-image are the parts of ego that are needed; without these we cannot live, but too much ego is not good. Ego can make us feel who we are, but it never teaches us who we really are. It is a false identification of mind and attached to cravings, desires, wants etc.

It is an outcome of the mind living in the past and future, which creates pain, suffering, and duality. Ego teaches that I am good and you are bad. All of these create separation and barriers within in the form of illusion and division. Ego closes our minds by limiting our belief systems with labels and judgments of our thoughts. Finally, it looks at others and creates chaos and turmoil, based on comparison and competition.

Deprogram and decondition your mind, and focus on the sensation of awareness of breath during meditation practice. Accept this moment, and surrender to the higher power with loving, forgiveness, kindness, and a feeling of non-duality in order to transcend ego.

A director of a school came to me; her complaint was that she had so much self-image and self-respect that she did not want to talk to the children. She thought that she was the director of the school and a powerful person; she did not want to interact and share with children. But she was wrong, because her work was to teach and take care of children. She had developed too much ego, which was separating her from the children. I requested her to practice living in the now and focus on the awareness of breath to transcend her ego, but her mind had already been conditioned and programmed for a long period of time. However, she practiced and incorporated my instruction in her activities of daily living for a few months, and her ego was transcended because she deprogrammed and deconditioned her mind. She came again to feel that she was one with the children, and she enjoyed interacting and sharing with the children more and more, which was wonderful.

Negative Emotions Come from Ego

Anger, jealousy, fear, and resentment are the product of ego, which can be neutralized with love, compassion, kindness, and forgiveness.

Ego comes when we live superficial lives, where people are dual in natures and also feel that they are powerful and dominant because they live with mind, not with heart; they think they know everything, but they do not know everything, and ego comes out. Nobody wants pain, conflicts, problems, and suffering, but we create these things when we are not living in the now. We can dissolve past experience when we transcend ego. Ego identification is very dangerous. The divine peace, inner beauty, and love cannot be with you as long as you are under the control of ego, but they can stay with you when you dissolve ego by living in the now.

When Buddha read more than a thousand books for enlightenment, he created a wall of ego and nothing happened; moreover, it became an obstacle on his path. But as soon as he focused on the awareness of breath in meditation practice, all ego was transcended which meant he unlearned what he had learned, and finally, he was enlightened.

If you surrender ego, it means you are in alignment and harmony with the Universe, and everything starts happening on its own because you are in the now. Mind is already dissolved because you have already released your inner force energy into the Universe, and the Universe is ready to take care of you.

Awareness burns ego, greed, jealousy, hatred, negativity, darkness etc. and it brings positivity, full of inner joy, and blissful experience of our lives.

We must look at things as they are, but how can you look at things as they are if you are under the control of ego? It is only possible when you decondition your mind and live with awareness. Only then, you can observe life as a life or death as a death, because you have already transcended ego and started to look at things as they really are. Ego tells you to see life only as a celebration, and that is the problem: it never tells you to see that death is also a celebration. See how ego is hell and darkness. We cannot live in the moment under the control of ego. Breath dissolves ego and helps us to live here and now.

"The moment when you are absolutely silent with nothingness, everything descends from beyond, unknown, and empty space."-Sanjeev Kumar

Chapter 6

A Stress-Free Life

We can have more than 65,000 thoughts in a day. More than 99.99 percent of them are useless and delusional, and they come from living in the past or future, which creates stress. Just for an example, if I start thinking about my wife and speculating that she is getting into a relationship with someone else at work, it would create doubt and confusion wherever I am; I would end up in stress from thinking too much about her without any proper reason because I have already disconnected with this beautiful moment, and I cannot focus on what I am doing, and it also decreases my productivity level.

Such stress also comes from overwork in an industry sector when you get too much pressure of work; therefore, just be relaxed and take a few focused, relaxed breaths instead of getting irritated and putting anger on someone else. Create a great space within to dissolve all these kinds of stress and remain in peace; then stress is no more, because you are living here right now, letting go of everything else.

Stress also happens when we are not able to handle situations because we have been leading a wrong pattern of life. We are busy with our lives and often disconnect with this divine moment. We want to satisfy all desires, which is impossible. We are living outside, and we cannot look within; all attachments push us outside, and finally, we lose our true selves in order to satisfy desires. Therefore, we are not able to know who we really are. Finally, stress comes out at the end in the form of anger, frustration, and fear.

Day and night shift changes affect our physical and mental health because of changes in our biological clocks, and finally, stress comes out. Unwanted thoughts create tensions, worries, and anxieties, which come from the past and thinking about future, planning, jobs, careers etc. in this moment. The more we take oxygenated air, the more we get rid of stress, because oxygenated air filters our ill thoughts and rejuvenates our lives, enabling us to live in the now.

Stress has nothing to do with the outside. It has something to do with inside, but we blame outside factors. It also takes place when something has happened in the past, may be a severe illness or trauma or accident, and we can keep on thinking about it and finally, stress comes out. We are thinking about the future—careers, jobs, opportunities, and businesses—which creates stress as well because we are living in the future in the form of dream, ambition, goal etc.

It does not matter how much stressed you are. All stress can be dissolved when you are focused on awareness of breath. You must practice it wherever you are—whether in the office, your house, or a playground—and you can let go of worry, anxiety, and pain very easily and move to the next level.

Do not forget to bring your awareness to the breath. It does not matter how many times you disconnect with the breath; keep coming to the breath in order to get rid of stressful situations, and incorporate this habit into your every activity is your practice. Gradually you will observe that the thoughts of stressful situations disappear and you get relaxed because you are becoming connected with the breath and disconnected from the useless thoughts of fear, memory, ambition etc. You will feel totally relaxed because the breath is a life-force energy that connects you to the Universe and brings bliss, joy, and happiness when you become mindful and aware of your life in the now, not of thoughts.

Stress is negative thought energy collected inside our minds. It creates pain, and therefore, we need to change and transfer this energy into a different form. It is already in the form of thoughts of fear, thoughts of the past, thoughts of ambition, thoughts of our workloads. We can go for laughing, dancing, jogging, gym workouts etc. May be we can go for creative work, like painting, artwork, photography, or whatever activity we like, because relaxation depends upon your interest and hobby as well. We can go to a swimming pool and feel relaxed.

Take a relaxed breath and rest after a certain interval of time would add great value to your work. I like writing books, but when I keep on writing for a longer period of time I get tired and my productivity level goes down. Therefore, I need to relax and take a deep breath after a certain period of time. Then I can produce productive thoughts, which can reduce my stress level so I can enjoy my work.

You can save your energy level when you take rest after certain period of time, and then you can use it for right purposes, which is called the energy conservation technique. As soon as we wake up from sleep, we feel fresh because we regain our energy level and all useless thoughts are already dissolved; wonderful, beautiful thoughts pop up into our minds. Therefore, if we relax and take rest after a certain interval of time, we can feel fresh and powerful. We have to live into this moment with a deep connection with nature such as mountains, rocks, oceans, rivers etc. in order to get rid of stress.

CHAPTER 7

Laughter Therapy

We must laugh from the heart, not from the mind. Laughter from the heart can take you to higher consciousness in order to attain true self, and then it is blissful. You can keep on laughing without any reason, which does not make any sense because you are not aware, alert, and conscious of it. While laughing, you are releasing stuck energy into the Universe, because whatever energy you have stored inside for the last few years needs an outlet to be released out into the Universe; then you can feel relaxed, calm, and quiet.

You can practice laughing and experience it in your daily life in order to understand it. While laughing, you do not think about the past and future but remain here right now. As soon as you finish laughing, you can feel that you empty your thoughts of desire, dream, ambition, success etc. you have already released repressed, and suppressed energy into the Universe, and finally you can feel light and relaxed in the now. You got connected with it by let go of worry, let go of fear, let go of everything. Moreover, you have dissolved negativity, and you are in a transcendental state. It is part of a dynamic meditation practice as well.

Never be serious at all, because seriousness is worse than death. Laughter is life, love, and light in the purest form. You can laugh like a kid with full of awareness, and it comes out of ignorance and innocence, full of curiosity. When children laugh, they can keep on laughing without any obstacles. Therefore, if you want to become childlike again, you can laugh with awareness into this moment. Finally, you can observe that anger, fear, jealousy etc. get dissolved, because all kinds of negative emotions keep on collecting inside us in the form of useless and unproductive thoughts.

In total laughter, the mind can disappear into no-mind because it is dance, fun, play etc. But not everybody can laugh in totality, because they are worried for tomorrow or the past. They have created many problems because they are living with attachments and desires, and while clinging to those, they cannot laugh. Most people live with mind, and they can only smile in order to impress others, which is fake because they are stuck with inner turmoil and noise. They cannot laugh, because they are looking in others, not within. Even if they laugh, you can feel some ego in their laughing because they are disconnected from existence, and their laughing is not deep but in the form of suffering. In a real deep laugh, the mind disappears. When real laughter happens, a bright luminous light starts spreading from the center of your heart toward your circumference—just as you throw a stone into a silent pond and ripples start moving toward the source.

Laughter is a great medicine and powerful treatment for stressed people or those who are suffering from depression. In your deep laughter, guilt, worry, wound etc. disappear.

Only human beings have the ability for laughing, not any animals but those who are connected with books, scriptures, beliefs etc. they have lost the capacity for total laughing because they are involved with collecting too much ego in the form of fake knowledge. They can be doctors, engineers, accountants etc. They can be good in their careers, but they are not people of awareness, alertness, and deep connection with nature, because they have not gone for an inner journey so far and have not experienced true being; therefore, they cannot laugh with totality. Those who are meditators, nature-loving people, live from moment to moment; they have the capacity for total laughter because they are more connected with true inner being.

I want people not to be serious but remain full of joy, bliss, and happiness, with total laughter to disconnect from mind in order to be blissful in nature.

Laughing, dancing, and singing are the activities in which the thinking mind stops. You cannot truly laugh and think at the same time. You can laugh while thinking, but it is just to impress others and it reflects your duality pattern of life because you are doing two things together. But as soon as you really laugh, mind disappears, and you are already there because you are the door of knowing. If you are dancing, the boundaries, the divisions, between you and dancing are lost—which is the same as in laughing, singing, and so on, because you stop thinking and are completely absorbed in this moment. You become the dancer and singer, and then who is dancing and who is singing? It is not you, but it is your lower self converted into higher or true self while dancing because there is no mind or thought.

Laughing releases stuck energy, but if you are suffering in intense pain, you cannot laugh, because you are trapped in inner turmoil and noise. It is good exercise to release our negative energy into the Universe; laughing is a dynamic meditation in which your negative-emotion energy comes out.

Laughing decreases stress hormones and increases serotonin. When we have a low level of serotonin, we are connected with depression, anxiety, headache, and insomnia. As soon as you start laughing, it refreshes, rejuvenates, and dissolves your mind and enhances your energy level. It puts you in a peaceful and silent state because you release stuck energy into the Universe, which finally reduces stress, worry, depression, and tension, so you end up living into this moment.

CHAPTER 8

The Art of Happiness

Whatever you do, if it comes out of awareness and grows out within you without any force from the core of the heart, it is creative, and finally it brings happiness. It depends upon your interests as well. If someone tells me to do accounts work, I can do it to fulfill my basic need, but I won't like it because I am forced to do it, so I can never be happy doing it. If my interest is to teach people, definitely I will go for it; I can be more happy and satisfied because I like it, and that adds great value to my work. If I like to play the piano, I can go for it rather than making money because playing with piano brings bliss, joy, and happiness to me and I can attract abundance as well.

Nature-loving people are happy because they are connected with ocean, water, mountain, rock etc. Nature always dissolves our mind into no-mind and brings freshness with purity; it makes our lives richer, deeper, and fuller because it brings bliss, joy, and ecstasy, along with abundance.

Freedom has ultimate value. You can feel and realize it when you live alone. You can get connected with nature easily, and basically you are not alone; all of existence is ready to take care of you, and you can enjoy the freedom of everything, you can think freely, and you can do whatever you like. You are just like a bird that can fly in the sky alone because it is free. Whatever decisions you take, they are yours because you are free. You can be millions times more happy when you do meditation and look within because you are fully present into this moment. Whenever dependency comes, it means you are stuck with others' decision making, and then you cannot be happy. All kinds of great works are done in peace, and peace is the result of inner happiness when you live alone with freedom.

Everything is state of mind, whether people want happiness or unhappiness. There are always two possibilities open for you; no matter how bad a situation is, you can be either happy or miserable. You can be happy when you are imprisoned, and you can be miserable in a palace. It is your choice. If I have too many problems on my journey, again, I have two options: I can be either happy or miserable, but it depends upon my choice. If I want to be happy, then I can be happy no matter how bad a situation is! Most of the enlightened teachers lived happily when they lived with the poor people on the street. Buddha was miserable when he was in a palace, but he was happy when he started living with poor people on the street.

Happiness Is What You Have Inside

We collect many material things to increase happiness, but they bring worry, anxiety, tension, and troubles at the end because all these things are outside; they push to live on the circumference and affect your innermost being, which is at the center. Therefore, we need to stop and try to look within to know who we really are, and that would probably increase our happiness. I never say that you have to renounce the world or leave your home and settle down in a forest to increase your happiness because that is useless and worthless; you need to remain wherever you are in the now.

Children are happy, plants are happy, birds are happy, all of nature is happy. The most ordinary things are happy, but extraordinary things are often unhappy. When you are extraordinary, you can observe everything with ego and overlook the ordinary things in your life because you cannot understand the beauty of the chirping of birds and you cannot see how beautiful trees are. You cannot play with water in a pool because you are extraordinary. You can lose touch with the existence and become miserable when you are extraordinary like many politicians, businesspeople or whosoever they are. You have developed too much ego as soon as you get power, and you are more miserable than ordinary people because you are busy with mind and overlook the beauty and bounty of nature. Not only that, you have not connected with the innermost being through the power of existence.

A happy person really cannot have much ego. If you want to be really happy, then become a dancer, singer, poet, farmer, musician, author, nature lover etc. You can be happier in these occupations because you are connecting with nature and feel bliss, inner joy, and happiness. Do not try to become a diplomat, politician etc. Most of them are unhappy people because they are connected with mind; they cannot live in peace, and they do not want others to live in peace.

Sharing Is Needed

Everything shares on the planet, whether they are living or nonliving things. Trees and plants also share. Our lives are possible because of them: plants give us oxygen, and we give them carbon dioxide back, and we get lots of food from them as well.

Whatever you have, you can share with people. If you are happy, you can share happiness with others. When you are at peace, you can share peace with people. Everyone wants happiness, but they are seeking it in the outside world. True happiness comes in a peace when you are detached from thoughts of the outer world and are more attached with the inner world. As soon as you go deeper and deeper in silence, you are getting in tune with nature. You can feel happy, but it is not easy, because the outer world tries to push you to live with ego, mind, attachment, desire etc. in the circumference, but real happiness is found at the center of being in meditation, where innermost being is already there. The closer you get to the innermost being, the happier you feel.

People are badly stuck with noises and chattering of mind, which create doubt, confusion, distraction etc. They end up in pain and suffering because they have lost their true selves in order to fulfill endless desires. Ultimately you get nothing at the end of life and realize that you have used your time, energy, and everything to fulfill your desires, which have no meaning at all. Not only that, they have already created a few diseases, which cannot be cured, finally you have lost everything. Although you have made material richness, it has no use at all because desire and money never bring happiness and peace in your life. Just imagine how many millions of beautiful moments of your life you have already wasted in order to make material richness.

Balance Between Materialism and Spiritualism

Life is full of fun, bliss, and peace, but we are confused and doubtful because we try to live in both paths, but we can live only with either a fullness of meditation practice or with material richness. It is our choice. You cannot live in both paths together; if you try, you are creating misery and suffering in your life. Again, pain is inevitable but suffering is optional. You can live with both of them only when you go for intense meditation practice by developing the middle path or equanimity, which needs a tremendous amount of persistence, perseverance, consistency, strong will power, and patience in your life. It is better to balance your life on the middle path.

You cannot live in peace and bliss once you go for material attachment; you will finally end up living in great pain, the way Buddha lived when he was in the palace. This is the common problem that we are facing because we have endless and limitless desires created by us because we are living by the mind, and mind takes us to memory, imagination, projection, idea, planning etc. Another property of mind is chattering and wandering, which connect us with too many material things and we end up in chaos and inner turmoil and finally ego comes out, which is false identification with detachment from the true self; therefore, it brings temporary satisfaction, but in the long run, we end up in great pain. Therefore, it is better to decondition our minds and live here right now by maintaining balance between spiritualism and materialism.

Basic necessity is required; it is needed, but on top of it, if we have too much material richness, there is nothing wrong in it, but most of us lose our peace of mind because we are too much attached to the material richness, so we cannot enjoy it. We have to learn the word *equanimity*. It means we need to detach from those thoughts of material richness through living into this moment, developing a middle path by creating a great space within to dissolve the attached thoughts. We can enjoy the middle path, which means balance between them. This is the common problem of people we are facing now.

"Live this moment intelligently, consciously, beautifully, and meditatively in order to make your life deeper, fuller, and richer." -Sanjeev Kumar

Silence Is Bliss

Silence is the result of a thoughtless awareness, where you can just observe and witness of all thoughts but never judge and label them. There is a full stop of chattering and wandering of mind, but witnessing is always there.

Truth can be experienced only in silence. It has no words, no thoughts, but it is the pure present state. Whatever you say, read, and listen may not be truth just because somebody has said it, but when you experience it in your life with profound understanding and investigation, then it is right, which happens when you are in the state of no-mind state.

Creativity comes out of silence, and silence is the outcome of inner emptiness. When you sit silently and just watch and observe your thoughts, a true silence happens because your whole life is watching your thoughts. There are two kinds of silence: one is a forced one, and the other is a relaxed one. Forced silence happens when we are forcing ourselves to be silent, which does not work because it is false silence and you are putting too much effort and pressure on yourself. Even if it happens just for the time being, you can start judging and labeling the thoughts again. Relaxed silence happens spontaneously and naturally when you go for meditation by letting go of all kinds of thoughts.

Suppose I am writing an article and there are several thoughts coming into my mind. If I judge them, then I cannot write down the article properly, because many thoughts are taking control over me in this moment. It would affect my work productivity by taking me into the past and future; there is a disturbance of the flow of writing, which blocks me from getting to the silent state. Therefore, we must go along with the flow. Let the traffic go on, let the water flow, let the season go on, let the Universe flow through you, but our whole practice is to observe and witness the thoughts, and gradually you will observe that there are miraculous things happening around you, because you are silent and mind has already disappeared. Then, there is powerful energy created inside with a great space within, and it dissolves all chattering and inner noises.

Real silence arises from the space between two thoughts while thinking or the space between two words while speaking; the space connects the right kinds of people in a different part of the Universe so they can understand the secret and mystery of life. Existence listens only to silence but not words, because words are meaningless, arbitrary, and delusion. It is better to connect with existence by remaining in silence, and then you can understand how existence works for you.

As long as you are under control of your mind, you cannot laugh because mind has to disappear for total laughing in order to be silent in this moment.

Great power comes when you are quiet and relaxed and move beyond mind by asking deep questions, letting go of fear, anger, worry etc. in order to live now. This is the time when you begin to awaken and know yourself. Illumination can take place; light starts coming into your life so there is no more darkness; good intentions start manifesting in your life. There is no illusion, separation, or barrier; only awareness is there. As soon as you identify your mind, there is memory, flashback etc. start coming on your path, and there is illusion in the form of labeling, judgment, and identification take place, we forget the true nature of being, and our silence is affected.

Silence Is Shared, Not Words

Buddha used to share his words through silence because he realized that words and languages are meaningless; you need to understand words through silence. His presence was so powerful that whoever came across him got changed because he used to emit powerful positive energy with emptiness. He used to share his words through silence by creating a great space within. Can we develop that kind of presence, which is free from pain, lust, desire, anger, fear, jealousy etc.? We can, but we have to live in the now and do meditation practice and internally cleanse as much as we can; our minds are full of illusionary thoughts that create confusion and doubt.

Only true silence can be shared because it conveys a real message. Right feeling and thoughts come from inner emptiness, which is powerful and productive because it originates from silence.

Whatever things are silent, they are always powerful in nature. The sun is silent, the moon is silent, and trees are silent. You can talk to nature and trees when you are synchronizing your frequency with them by remaining in silence, but the problem with us is that we live with mind, which means there is a continuous chattering.

Mind is full of projections, dreams, desires, and expectations, which never let you remain in silence; as soon as you quiet and witness of those thoughts, you become silent.

All that you have to do is to go deeper in meditation, beyond mind into silence. No thoughts, no emotions, no moods, just a silent watchfulness and waiting for whatever existence finds ready for you. Impatience and restlessness create a problem in you because you are not silent; moreover, you have created turmoils and inner noises, and you are badly stuck inside, which creates problems in your life. It does not matter how much turmoils and noises in the form of anger, fear, hatred etc. you can overcome them through meditation, and then courage develops by remaining in silence. Ego creates too much turmoils and inner noises in the form of negative emotion because you are under the control of mind; you need to go beyond mind in order to become silent. In your silence, all questions will disappear, all problems will be gone, and you will be just an observer and watcher.

In meditation, silence comes on its own accord while watching and witnessing of thoughts without any struggle and fight, and that is your blissfulness; it is your own fragrance, which you never knew before because you were full with too much noises and turmoils. It is pure space and no-mind state, where desire, dream, ambition, and goal are released. If you really want to share the truth with people, just remain silent and let the people get connected with one another without words. That's the only way truth has been shared—from one blissful heart to another blissful heart. If you really want to experience miracles, then remain silent and everything else follows on its own accord.

As soon as you reach the deepest level of meditation, a tremendous silence, peace, and blissfulness arise within you, which can take you to the beyond, unknown, and empty space; from there you can understand the secret of life because your frequency is aligning with the Universe.

Truth comes to those who are awake, mindful, alert, and aware and living in the now. You do not need to go anywhere; just open your eyes with awareness. It comes and it comes at the right time; be patient and do not be in a hurry, or you will miss it. Do not search, seek, and find it because it is already there. This is the eternal law. It is better to be silent to get the answers of all questions.

You can merge, share, and meet in silence with existence.

"Do not be afraid of experiencing of all duality: dark and light, good and bad, positive and negative. It adds great value to your life." -Sanjeev Kumar

CHAPTER 10

Nature Is Divine

Nature is formless, limitless, boundless, and infinite, and it vibrates at the highest level. It brings everything in our lives, but we create obstacles in the form of too much ego. As we know, nature is always available to us in the form of water, sunlight, mountain, air etc. First of all, we must have gratitude for this because it is the gift of nature. We are here because of it.

Huge Trust with Nature Is Required

You must not try to control any situation; let it be controlled by itself because whatever happens, it happens for a good reason. If you are honest, truthful, and pure, nothing wrong will take place; you can trust in nature. If you have right intention, then right things will happen to you, so just live in the moment by surrendering and letting go of everything, no matter how bad the problem is. Nature will take care of you.

This means dropping all struggle, fight, aggression, dream, imagination, ambition, and success. And when you drop all these things, suddenly you become aware that the ego has disappeared and you have moved to the next level, but again, great trust in nature is required.

Nature Is Beyond Everything

We spend our whole lives earning money and end up in frustration because we are more connected with material needs; problems come out when we forget true selves, which are already in us. One's innermost being cannot be discovered by material ways, but it can be explored by deeply connecting with nature, and it brings inner peace, which is beyond everything. Those who are connected with material richness suffer badly at the end of life because they cannot discover their true selves. It is better to balance our lives.

Blissful People Live in Nature

The energy of people who live with nature is highly creative. There are different kinds of people who live with nature, like fishers, woodcutters, farmers, sailors etc. They are really unique people because they are always connected with water, trees, mountains, oceans, and rivers. They are really fresh, trustworthy, honest, and authentic people because they spend their whole lives with the beauty of nature; therefore, their consciousness level is higher and richer.

Beauty of Nature

One can enjoy with the beauty of nature. When you are deeply engrossed in listening to good music, a deep absorption takes place. You forget about your self, you are drowned in the sweet sound of music, you start living in the now, and you can experience the moment of peace and beauty of nature around you. The same process occurs while singing; when you sing, you forget about yourself that you are singing. You are deeply absorbed in the sweet melody of singing, and you become one with the singing. Here the singer becomes singing, and in that moment you can feel the beauty of nature and bliss.

Conspiracy of Nature

People come into our lives to share their thoughts and move away. Sometimes nature may connect you with the wrong person, but when you are right and honest, right things happen to you at the end. This is just because of the conspiracy of nature.

Everything keeps on moving—like the earth moves on, the sun moves on, the stars move on—because you are looking outside, but there is something within you that never moves on; it is eternally eternal, and it gets deeply connected with true nature, which is the innermost being. The question comes, how can we reach to that point? It is only through deep connection with nature.

Life becomes blissful only through the heart, because it is directly connected with nature—never through the mind. The mind creates logic, science, intellectual gamble, ego, and duality, but the heart creates love, bliss, truth, freedom, and awareness, and the heart is directly connected through nature.

CHAPTER 11

Let Go and Surrender

All expectation leads into frustration because expectation means desire and desire means attachment with ego, which is never fulfilled; the problems come out when people keep on expecting more and more. Ultimately they lose everything whatever they had before. When you expect nothing, then you get everything, but when you expect everything, then you get nothing in your life. It works based on what we think, guided by the law of attraction in the Universe. When people are forcing you to expect something, it is even worse because force always create resistance. When you relax and are totally relaxed, you get everything in your life without any expectation. This is only possible when you let go of everything and deeply connect with the Universe in this moment.

Profound trust to the innermost being and listen to your inner voice without effort, with no more struggles. Surrender deeply to within, and then you can let go of worry, let go of tension, let go of anxiety, let go of the future, and finally, let go of everything. Then you can observe that you got rid of all thoughts of past and future and remain here right now with awareness.

Let the Universe Flow Through Us

Don't try to fight with nature. You must know how to relax with nature by letting go. Flow with nature and allow nature to possess you totally; in that way, you disappear and you are not. The moment you find you are not, light enters in you and empties all thoughts of past and future. You are then very close to the innermost being because you are filled with light by emptying yourself of all useless thoughts. There is no space left over for any thoughts because you have already let go of everything. In that moment, only pure awareness is there, in which truth arrives.

We must let things happen on their own accord; we must let the Universe flow through us and make it happen. You need to surrender—that's all—and just think that whatever is going to happen, it is going to happen for good reason. Try to listen and connect with existence only when you are silent and let go of all thoughts of past and future. There is no stress, no memory, no ambition, no success; you need to drop everything and stop fighting with existence, and finally, you will become witness of everything. You do not have any thoughts left over, but move away and create a great space that dissolves everything.

Whenever it happens, you can observe the sunrise and the sunset. The sunset is so beautiful and overwhelming that you can forget the past and the future, all your desires; you can forget all lust, pleasure, and pain, and only the present remains. You are one with the moment; there is no observer, and no one is going to be observed. The observer becomes the observed.

Deep Connection With Existence

Don't force anything; become one with existence and let life flow into this moment in a letting-go state, and then nature will start opening millions of flowers without forcing the buds. Do not be in a hurry and lose patience, but be relaxed and total relax into this moment. The sun is going to rise and flowers are going to start emitting their fragrance; be patient, and everything falls into the right place. Don't show agitation and fight with existence, or you are going to lose this blissful moment of your life. Just be there and observe and witness of whatever is happening here and now; be alert and awake. You can surrender and trust within. Basic things are needed, for example, food, shelter, and cloth. You cannot live without these things but still you can relax, and in that relaxing, the truth happens. The whole purpose of living in this world with a letting-go attitude and deep trust within is to sit under a tree and do nothing, the way Buddha did.

Inner Achievement Through Surrender and Letting Go

There are two kinds of achievement in our lives. One is inner, which is related to peace, joy, and happiness; the other is an outer one, full of material success. If you want to achieve the outer one, you need to be desperate, competitive, violent, and aggressive; but when you are looking for the inner one, you need to drop the idea of fighting, competitiveness, violence, and aggressiveness. Whatever you can achieve in the state of working hard and struggling, you can achieve a hundred times more than that by living into this moment, letting go of everything, and relaxing into this moment.

Forget everything about the past, disconnect yourself completely, and don't look back at all because looking back is a great sin and illusion. Look in the now and be in a totally relaxed state with awareness, and then everything is available to you. That availability makes you valuable presence!

There is deep intense pain that happens as a result of loss of family members, accidents, trauma, severe illness etc. We must not escape from it because it is fact and reality; rather, we have to accept it by going deeply and face it with great courage. Experience it, but do not fear it at all. Enjoy it completely, but do not let mind take control over you; try to connect with the awareness of breath in order to live in the now. For example, maybe you could have prevented this situation if you were there, but it is useless to think about it because that moment has already gone!

"In order to be aligned with the frequency of the Universe, you need to think in terms of energy, frequency, and vibration."-Sanjeev Kumar

CHAPTER 12

Fear and Overcome It

Fear is a part of the negative emotion that takes place when we are not in the moment; something has happened in the past, and we keep on thinking about the past in the form of memory and flashback, which creates fear in this moment. Fear happens when we are not able to discover who we really are by living on the circumference.

Fear is the result of unwanted and illusionary thoughts, and it always comes from unknown space. Everybody has fear, and fear of death is the ultimate fear. All other fears are secondary. Most of the thoughts are unreal; they have no meaning at all, and finally they create fear.

For an example, I had too much fear a few days back that I would fail in examination, and finally, I failed in them because I had too many irrational and illogical thoughts of fear of failures. I wasted a lot of time and energy on them without any reason. It happened because too many thoughts of the past and the future in the form of fear interfered with this moment. There is always something that is holding you back in your life that makes you unsuccessful. It is the greatest obstacle on the path of human growth and development.

It happens with everyone in their day-to-day lives if they do not live with awareness. Finally, it decreases their productivity level. Therefore, whenever it happens to you, just bring the focus of awareness of breath at the top of the nostrils to live in the now, and then fear is no more.

Here is another example. What would you do if someone put a gun to your head? You must accept this moment fully in order to remain here in the now and act wisely to protect yourself from him; as soon as you deny this moment and try to escape in the form of argument, discussion, conflict etc. maybe it ends with fighting and bad consequences because the argument takes you into the past or future. So he might shoot and harm you.

Fear Can Be Understood and Then Be Overcome

Fear arises when we are uncertain, doubtful, and afraid of losing our jobs, money etc. For an example, when students prepare for an examination, they think that they might fail in the examination; they are fearful, it does not matter how intelligent they are, and finally, they fail because fear overcame them. Moreover, they live in the future and are afraid that they cannot pass, and finally, they fail.

Most thoughts are useless, unproductive, and delusional. The more we have unwanted and delusionary thoughts, the greater amount of fear appears in our lives.

There are two kinds of fear. One is positive, and the other one is negative.

An example of positive fear is, if you do not study hard, you cannot pass the examination. You have fear of failure that you cannot pass the examination, therefore you study, work hard, and prepare well. This is called positive fear. You cannot be a good doctor if you do not study much; since you need to study hard in order to be a good doctor, there is a fear attached with you, and it is called positive fear.

Everybody fails, but there are some people who consider it is an opportunity to learn, grow, and evolve. Fear of failure leads to success because it helps you to move to the next level and discover your hidden potential. The more you live here right now, the more you can discover your potential because you are moving away from the past and future.

The second kind of fear is negative fear—you fear that you cannot pass the examination no matter how intelligent you are and how hard you work. This is an unproductive and useless fear, which is created within you; it is worse because it brings negativity and darkness into your life. It impairs your wisdom and knowledge. It blocks you from growth and development. When you are going for entrepreneurship, you may have a fear of failure that you cannot be successful because negative fear is taking control of you and ruin everything in your life. Maybe you are not going to take risks. This negative fear holds you back and discourages you from starting a business because you are moving into the future.

Can you fight with fear? Never; you cannot fight with it. Just bring courage and love in and focus on the breath, and then there is no fear. It is the same with darkness—you cannot fight with it; you need to bring light in, and then there is no darkness.

If fear arises, accept it, but never fight with it; otherwise, the problems will be more complex. You can understand fear only by moving down into the center of being. As soon as you live on the circumference, you are full of ego, and ego creates all fear because ego is attached with us.

Desire Is Part of Ego

Fear is the result of endless desires, which comes from the past and the future. All desires come from attachment, and finally, attachment creates fear. When you have too many material desires, you try to satisfy them by focusing your energy level onto them, missing the innermost being because you are living superficially with all distractions. You spend your whole life on the circumference because you cannot move into the center of being. You are lost outside and end up creating too much fear because you are attached with endless material desires. The innermost being is available in this moment, which you are missing.

Never suppress and repress fear whenever it happens; let it happen with full intensity because it teaches you the depth of fear. Although you know about it but you have not experienced it. Watch it with awareness, face it boldly, and counter it by moving deep down into the center of being. You may tremble, shake, and perspire because you have not experienced it before. But gradually, the more your eyes become clear, the more your awareness becomes alert and sharp, and the more your consciousness becomes transparent, fear will disappear like a cloud in the sky. And once fear disappears, you are already there with total presence.

When you love more, fear disappears. Therefore, a question comes: Why can't we put forth the same energy for love? As soon as we put forth the same energy for love, fear is no more because a shift of energy takes place, and we must pay more attention to love. Once you realize that the presence of love becomes the absence of fear, your life becomes bliss.

Meditation can overcome fear. It discovers who you really are. As soon as you know who you really are, then there is no fear, because you can turn actuality into potentiality; fear is present only when we live superficially. The best way to dissolve fear is to have a deep connection with trees, the rivers, the mountains, and the stars—the whole Universe—because all of these put you in this moment. Take the whole beauty and bounty of nature inside you, and then you can reach to the center of being, where fear is no more.

"Silence is the source of all power, and it shares the words. Become silent like sunshine and water." -Sanjeev Kumar

CHAPTER 13

True Courage

Courage is one of the positive emotions that arises when we move into unknown space. The more you live in the now, the more you become courageous. Buddha had the courage to go for meditation for thirty days under the Bodhi tree continuously, and he finally defeated all evil illusionary thoughts through meditation practice with persistence, great determination, and tremendous courage; finally, he got enlightenment. We must have great courage to defeat the inner world, which consists of thoughts of fear, thoughts of delusion, thoughts of anger, thoughts of hatred etc. Basically these are useless and purposeless thoughts that come from living in the past and future in the form of delusion; these are main obstacles on the path of growth and development. Great courage is needed to defeat the inner world, not the outer world!

Sometimes these thoughts are present in the form of dream, imagination, projection, flashback etc. inside, which create problems in our lives, but as soon as you live in the now, you can defeat them very easily, as the way Buddha overcome them!

Jesus Christ had the courage to go for teaching and preaching for his whole life, and he healed millions of lives. If you really want to be courageous, then first of all you must be honest and truthful and have deep trust in yourself. Most of the great teachers have immense courage to look within in order to discover hidden potential. Courage comes in when you deal with unknown, and more of it comes when you live here right now.

As you fail many times in any project, great courage comes in when you let go of fear, let go of failure, let go of anger, and let go of memory and move to the next level although you may have committed many mistakes in the past. When you keep on dwelling on all those mistakes, then you cannot overcome them, so it is better to let go of all mistakes and move to the next moment in order to live in the now with great courage. The same situation arises when students prepare for examinations. It is very hard to move to the next moment because past failure starts affecting them into this moment, so it is better to let go of mistakes whatever they have and move to the next moment.

Only courageous people can enjoy their lives because they have curiosity to know the unknown and beyond. They can be discoverer and explorer no matter how many times they fail in their lives. Existence takes care of them, but as I said, they must be honest, authentic, and truthful, and then everything falls into the right place.

The true reflection of a human being is not seen in running water. It is only seen in stagnant water. Our minds work like water. They run in waves and circles of thoughts, not allowing us to see the truth as it is. Once you calm your mind to stillness, you can see the truth exactly as it is. Courage comes from the center of being, but great courage is needed. We all need quiet and still minds, and then everything will happen rightly. If your mind is full of inner turmoil, confusion, doubt, hatred, anger, fear etc. it will be an obstacle on the path to true or higher self. The real courage comes in when you are in silence, with no control of mind, and let go of all these thoughts of past and future.

You are struggling and fighting and getting lost every time because you are living outside on the periphery, where everything is dual and full of ego. Great courage is needed to discover the true self, where duality and ego of mind can be dissolved. It is possible when you are living in the now, and finally, struggling and fighting are over.

The true meaning of courage is to live with heart. It is an absence of fear. Courage is an outcome of looking within and remaining here right now. It always takes you beyond body, mind, and soul. Because it discovers your hidden potential, it guides you within through inner voice and teaches you to take risks. A courageous person is always blissful in nature.

It is true that there is survival for the best in nature, but only those survive who are truly courageous, because existence takes care of them and they are deeply connected with nature, not with the mind. The time when you go deeper and deeper into stillness, you start becoming more courageous because you are getting rid of all inner and outer noises. The more courageous you are, the more you go toward the center of your being, where stillness speaks through you, and then you can observe that all the factors that are obstacles on your path are already dissolved. Now you are free from all attachment, ego, mind, desire, greed, memory, imagination, projection, dream, planning etc.

Discoverers and explorers are courageous people. In spite of several failures, they discovered everything, and we are here because of them. Whosoever has done extraordinary things in his or her life was a highly courageous person. All people have courage, but they are unaware about it because they live in the past and future.

The fewer thoughts you have, the more courageous you are because you are fully present in this moment but move deeper and deeper. The more relaxed you become, the more possibilities there are that you can get connected with higher self and you can overcome fear as well.

The Universe is a great source energy that carries the highest power, but we are not connected with it, because we are living in delusion and are lost. As soon as we get connected with it by moving deep down within, then fear is no more, because we are one with source energy.

CHAPTER 14

Anger and Overcome It

Anger is created when we are not alert, aware, conscious, and awake. It arises when we identify and condition our minds in the form of ego. Ego is present superficially, but as soon as ego gets hurt for any reason, anger comes out.

Anger is impermanent and unreal, a part of negative emotion. It happens when you overreact to a situation by not living into this moment; it happens as soon as you lose focus on the awareness of breath.

Whenever this happens, we have to turn our awareness inside without judgment and never react to anger at all. If people create anger in you, it is better to create a gap, which means that only after one day or a few hours, you reply back to them. Most of the anger comes from living in the past or future; therefore, just look at what is happening in the now, and do not try to escape from it. It is negative-emotion energy created inside, which can be dissolved as soon as you sit on the bank of an ocean or river and take fresh oxygenated air. You can realize that the intensity of the anger has gone down. As you move deeper and deeper, there is light and love at the center of being. Peace comes as anger disappears.

When anger arises, just sit silently and observe; watch it as a silent watcher. Be alert and listen to the message of it; investigate and introspect it within, and maintain a distance from it. The more you maintain a distance from it, the better you are.

Focus your total attention and energy on it for deep understanding. What is the root cause of anger? From where did it come, and how did it happen? How can we overcome it, and how can it affect our lives? Our awareness gets sharper and deeper the more we try to understand it. The more you understand it, the sooner anger will disappear; the more you meditate on it, the less anger you will have, and finally, peace and silence will happen. Never repress anger; if you repress it, this anger can be shared or transferred from one person to another person and end up in more anger.

Shift Energy from Anger to Creativity

Anger is only on the surface; when you go deep inside the anger at the bottom level, you are full of energy that you never knew before. This energy is not active because it is not used, but it is creative potential energy. We need to turn this energy into creativity. Forget about anger as a problem; transfer the energy of anger into the energy of creativity, which may be in the form of dancing, music, photography, reading, singing, painting, sports, games etc. and gradually anger will disappear. For example, while dancing you put total energy in the movement of different body parts, which result into conversion of energy of anger into energy of dancing and you feel tired, relaxed, and finally anger is released.

Take a few relaxed breaths whenever you get angry and live here right now. Create a great space within to dissolve anger. Whenever anger happens, let it happen; feel, taste, and meditate on it. Go deep down and experience it. As you move deeper and deeper, you can enjoy with it by witnessing, watchfulness, and observation; therefore, become an observer and watcher.

Anger is necessary; it brings bliss and inner joy because it is another side of the same coin. Can you love someone else without anger? No, you cannot do it, because when you love others, the anger comes out at the end because light cannot exist without darkness; therefore, love cannot exist without anger.

A friend of mine told me that he gets angry at some of his friends because they bring their own anger upon him. I told him that if you are a deep meditator then you can experience the taste and flavour of their anger by remaining mindful, alert, and awake. But if not then, you would create more anger because you may overreact with them. They are not meditators, and if you get angry at them, it means every person is in anger. But still you can ignore their anger as well by creating a great space within during meditation practice.

The situation is very simple. My friend provided enough room to be angry at all of them because they are not aware and conscious of it, and finally ended up creating more anger, which led to turmoil.

This is my message. If you are a meditator, then you must be an observer and watcher; it does not matter that your friends or others bring their own anger at you. If you become angry, it means you are not aware, alert, and conscious, and then the anger has appeared from both ends.

"Miracle is the result of internal cleansing."- Sanjeev Kumar

CHAPTER 15

The Power of Creativity

Creativity means loving whatever you do, following your heart—enjoying, celebrating, and fun that comes from within without force. It just flows with nature when you are very close to existence. It is the outcome of inner space. Creative people are poets, writers, painters, photographers etc. who are totally merged with existence. They live in the now while doing any activities. For example, when you are painting or drawing a picture, the more you focus in this moment, the better your creativity is. Just imagine that when you are thinking about wife, kids, work etc. while painting; you cannot depict creativity because you are not there; you are living in the future, and therefore, your creativity can be affected.

Creativity is just noticing, witnessing, and observation of thoughts, but not labeling or judgment of those thoughts. Whatever thoughts may be good or bad, positive or negative, are coming into this moment; just witness them, but do not judge them at all because judgment can take you into the past and the future. We can learn from past mistakes, but don't dwell on them; then move into the now. The past and the future lose all power of creativity, and we have no control over thinking.

Mind means thinking, but discovery, exploration, and innovation always take place in this moment. We can put total energy into this moment by just focus on the awareness of breath. When we are fully relaxed and let go of everything, disconnecting with the past and the future, then we can observe that beautiful and wonderful thoughts pop up in our brains from beyond, the empty, and unknown space, as soon as we get connected with nature—the ocean, mountain, rock etc.—because it dissolves and deconditions our minds.

We can lose our power of creativity when we read many religious books, scriptures etc. The more you read, the more you lose creativity, because creativity is already within; the more you explore and try to know yourself by looking inside, the more creative you become. Reading many books brings too much ego, and it separates us from creativity. Not only that, it takes us into the past and the future, which disconnects us from this moment. If you want to be really creative, then live alone and try to connect with nature by letting go of all thoughts— just witness them. As soon as you connect with people's mind, they create problem, pain, and suffering, and again creativity is lost.

Force Destroys Creativity

Follow your heart rather than mind in order to be creative. For example, if you have a passion and interest to go for playing music, you can have fun and enjoy it. You can play in your own way. Maybe you could show an inner reflection of beautiful thoughts in a form of creativity and positive emotions, which is different from others. You can do some discovery on it because you love it from the core of your heart, and definitely it brings abundance to your life. If your passion and interest is for photography, then you must go for it in your own way. You could bring some creative ideas of taking images at a different angle than others because photography is your passion and you love it from your heart. Definitely you put your total energy into it, which is creativity, and it raises your productivity.

If someone forced you to go for playing with football, maybe you would not like it because your interest and passion is photography, but still you play with it because someone forced you to do so. This means you will not be creative. Force destroys creativity, and it brings resistance as well. You can discover creativity only when you are here in the now and follow your heart with effortless effort and relax into this moment. When you dance, try to bring total energy to it, which is different from others. That means your dancing activity is unique from others. When you follow others, then you are not creative. Do not look in others but be yourself and look within. If you laugh in your own way, then it is creative because it is different from others; that means you are reflecting your inside beauty of heart in the form of laughing. Never follow and look in others. Creative people live in silence and are fully absorbed in this moment.

You can laugh in a creative way. You can clean the house in a creative way. You can clean your clothes in a creative way. You can prepare food in a creative way. Your deep presence in every activity is needed. Even if you do nothing and sit silently just witnessing of your thoughts, that is more creative, the same way as Buddha did.

Never condition your mind in order to be creative, but decondition and deprogram it. Conditioning limits your brain and belief system, and finally, it destroys creativity; therefore, live with nature, water, and fresh air.

Creativity is lost as soon as goals, ambitions, and dreams arise; an ambitious person cannot be creative. Ambitious people do not live in the now, and they do not love any activities either; they just do them to fulfill their desires with force and accomplish a goal for popularity and fame. They put conditions on everything based on give-and-take relationships. Not only that, they have too many attachments and clinging; they are full of planning to get first prize in any competition because they need fame. Their intention is to connect with material attachments and waste every moment of life living in the future; therefore, they are wasting time and energy without any reason. They are teaching the same things to whosoever is connected with them and making others' lives miserable because they lost their creativity.

CHAPTER 16

The Miracle of Existence

The whole secret of life is to understand how existence works. The more you become still and look within, the better you will come to know your true self in order to reach to the center of being. The whole power of the Universe is within you. You need to just unfold it with a deep connection to existence and listen to your inner silence, which is possible by living in the now, just witnessing of thoughts. Never listen to and look in others, but follow your heart, remaining in silence in the form of intuition, because only heart can connect you with existence, not the mind.

Always listen to your inner voice within and follow wherever it leads you, but remain silent and then you can hear stillness. Be spontaneous and natural, with deep trust, by disconnecting with the outer world completely. This is thoughtless silence, but full of awareness. You are utterly relaxed. You are no longer in the state of deep sleep; you are awake, conscious, and more alert than ever. This is the only way to have a deep connection with existence.

Whosoever is deeply connected with existence, their life is full of awareness, and their death is also full of celebration because they disappear into absolute nothingness. When Buddha died, his death was full of celebration. He had lived his entire life in a peaceful, joyful, and silent way;

and whosoever were present during his time of death, they were enlightened because powerful meditative energy had released into the Universe. He lived and died in meditation. His life was just like a mirror: whoever came in front of him, he just reflected, because he was completely empty. If you have nothing and come in front of a mirror, you reflect nothing. Because there is nothing to reflect.

The higher you rise, the more you can see everything with awareness. Then there is no past and no future but only the present. Confusion is dissolved and clarity comes out; you can laugh or dance or cry, in which each atom of the body parts move and become one with existence. In order to listen to existence, you need to be silent, calm, and relaxed. But generally we go through affirmations, which means repetition of a mantra or anything else again and again, which is wrong because it conditions our minds by repeating the same thoughts—but we need to decondition our minds by creating thoughtless space within and emptying all kinds of thoughts. Affirmation is just the opposite of awareness.

INDEX

M

N

BLOG

1. Wisdom of a Lotus Flower

The roots of the lotus flower are always in the mud and grow through the deep-water level, rises up to the surface of the water. It blooms in the sunlight, but mud is needed for real growth of the lotus flower; just as darkness is important for light, negativity is important for positivity. The real growth of the human being takes place in a negative situation, like a lotus flower; when it grows, it never touches the mud. This growth is real, divine, and upward. Therefore, if we want to evolve and attain higher bliss, we should live with negative and unaware people but never allow them to enter our own space.

2. The Power of Nothingness

Nothingness is a state of thoughtless awareness as a result of witnessing and observation of thoughts. They end up in a vacuum formation, in which old energy moves out and fresh energy moves in on autopilot, which can empty all of your thoughts, achieving a state of emptiness or hollowness. The final purpose of meditation is to create nothingness.

TESTIMONIALS

"Inspiring and Rejuvenating"- Life transforming workshop. It connected to my mind, body, and soul.

—Jonathan, Professor (Canada)

The course on "The Power of the Present Moment" has helped me to explore and realize my full potential.

—John Milton, Doctor (America)

I used to attend his discourses on "Mindfulness Training." I have learned many facts about mindfulness. It enhanced my wisdom.

—Tom Jay, Director (Canada)

Sanjeev ignited my mind with passion. It was amazing and mind-blowing. It made a great difference in my life.

—D. Smith, Teacher (America)

I had been suffering from anxiety and depression for the last few years. Sanjeev taught me about meditation and deep connection with nature, which has really helped me to get rid of it.

—Jay Nicholson, Professor (Germany)

I had much anger and fear in my life. As soon as I attended his discourse on emotional wellness, I got transformed and transcended fear and anger.

—Marina Cathy, University Student (Canada)

I used to live in the past and the future, which has created many problems in my life. A few days back, I attended his workshop. I learned many ways to live into this moment.

—Brenda Macdonald, Scientist (Australia)

I am a director of a school. I had tremendous ego. I never used to interact with students properly. As soon as I started attending his discourses about "How to Transcend Ego" my life got transformed and transcended ego.

—Lawrence, Doctor (Canada)

UPCOMING BOOK
AND CMRC (CENTER)

Mindfulness Is the Way of Life

Mindfulness is the ability to observe things as they really are without any prejudice or judgment, which is also called nonjudgmental awareness. It also observes the deep and true nature of everything into this moment. It observes things profoundly without concepts, dogmas, beliefs, and opinions. This sort of deep observation leads to a complete absence of confusion about the real nature of things.

Canadian Mindfulness Research Center
(www.santeaching.com)

The Canadian Mindfulness Research Center is a place where you can share your wisdom to grow, based on discovery, self-exploration, meditation, and a deep connection with nature. The whole purpose of education is transformation, based on learning, sharing, and evolution.

Courses offered for workshops and retreats

1- Mindfulness is the way of life
2- The power of meditation
3- Thoughts are things
4- The power of present moment
5- The power of nothingness
6- Live our life through heart versus mind
7- Nature is divine
8- Let go and surrender
9- Stillness speaks
10- Transcend fear and anger
11- Stress free life
12- Transcend ego
13- Art of happiness
14- Laughter therapy

You can contact him for workshops, retreats, and presentation. His website-www.santeaching.com or email- sanjeev@santeaching.com

CPSIA information can be obtained
at www.ICGtesting.com
Printed in the USA
LVOW12s1945111116
512670LV00001B/9/P